# Terraform for Developers

*Essentials of Infrastructure Automation and Provisioning*

AF271572

*Kimiko Lee*

Published by: GitforGits
Publisher: Sonal Dhandre
www.gitforgits.com
support@gitforgits.com

Printed in India

First Printing: July 2023

ISBN: 978-8196288341

Cover Design by: Kitten Publishing

For permission to use material from this book, please contact GitforGits at support@gitforgits.com.

# Prologue

"Unlock the power of Infrastructure as Code and propel the career forward as a professional Terraform developer with the help of this comprehensive guide - 'Terraform for Developers'. This book serves as the roadmap to understand, implement, and master the concepts and complexities of Terraform.

Terraform, a product by HashiCorp, is a widely used open-source tool that allows developers and infrastructure professionals to manage and orchestrate their infrastructure through code. It provides a uniform language that enables you to describe and provision the entire infrastructure's lifecycle. The adoption of Terraform by many organizations worldwide stands testament to its capabilities, transforming the way we approach infrastructure management.

'Terraform for Developers' offers an all-inclusive understanding of Terraform, meticulously designed for developers, system administrators, and DevOps professionals. The book is sectioned into ten chapters, each focusing on a specific aspect of Terraform, ensuring you a step-by-step walk through its complexities. The book begins by grounding you in the fundamentals of Terraform, elucidating the core concepts and its architecture. We then explore the process of setting up Terraform in different environments, highlighting crucial aspects such as installation, configuration, and security. A thorough comprehension of the Terraform lifecycle is indispensable to the journey, from initialization to plan, apply, and resource destruction.

Once grounded in the basics, the book ventures into advanced topics, unveiling the essential components of a Terraform project. We will acquire the know-how of working with variables, outputs, provisioners, and modules to organize and modularize the code. We will learn how to efficiently handle errors, maximize performance, and keep a check on the Terraform code's quality. We delve into Terraform's networking capabilities, guiding you on managing Virtual Private Clouds (VPCs), subnets, routing, and load balancers. We will understand how to automate scaling to manage traffic influx. Also, we explore how to handle secrets using Azure Key Vault, showcasing the importance of secure secrets management in modern infrastructure.

The latter part of the book explores the process of testing in Terraform, presenting how to implement unit, integration, validation, and compliance testing. Alongside, we discuss the power of Terraform in a CI/CD environment, a crucial factor in the DevOps world today. The book concludes with advanced topics like managing Kubernetes resources, generating dynamic secrets with HashiCorp Vault, and provisioning Azure Kubernetes Service (AKS) cluster.

In each chapter, practical examples and detailed explanations accompany theoretical concepts, transforming complex Terraform topics into digestible knowledge chunks. We will get the hands dirty, writing Terraform configurations, managing resources, testing the infrastructure, and more.

By the end of the journey with 'Terraform for Developers,' you will have acquired a deep understanding of Terraform and its applications. We will have the confidence to build, change, and version the infrastructure efficiently and safely. Whether you're a beginner looking to get started with Terraform or an experienced professional aiming to deepen the understanding, this book has something valuable for you. So, buckle up, roll up the sleeves, and let us dive into the world of Terraform together!"

# Content

# Preface

"Terraform for Developers" provides a comprehensive guide to mastering infrastructure as code with Terraform, intended for both beginners and experienced practitioners. The book starts by introducing foundational Terraform concepts like its architecture, setup on various cloud platforms, and the syntax of its configuration language HCL. This grounds the reader in core skills needed to author infrastructure code.

It then explores the full lifecycle of a Terraform project from state management, provisioning, networking, troubleshooting errors, and testing practices. Each phase is explained through practical examples relevant to real-world usage. Advanced skills like performance optimization, CI/CD integration, and modules are covered to take the reader from basic to expert. The book finishes with sophisticated use cases like Kubernetes infrastructure automation and secrets management with HashiCorp Vault.

The end result is a 360-degree education in Terraform - from installation to advanced usage across public clouds. Readers gain both theoretical foundations and hands-on skills transferred through practical examples. The book takes a holistic approach that equips practitioners to leverage Terraform in production environments.

In this book you will learn how to:

- Comprehensive introduction to Terraform's architecture, syntax, and semantics.
- Practical examples to understand Infrastructure as Code (IaC) concept.
- Detailed guidance on setting up Terraform in diverse environments.
- Exploring Terraform's lifecycle, from initialization to resource destruction.
- Insightful exploration of error management and troubleshooting techniques.
- In-depth discussion on network management using Terraform for real-world scenarios.
- Advanced topics coverage like Kubernetes resources and dynamic secrets.
- Detailed explanation of Terraform's integration with CI/CD pipelines.
- Extensive study of Terraform testing, including unit, integration, and compliance tests.
- Knowledge on module creation and version control for efficient code reuse.

# GitforGits

## Prerequisites

"Terraform for Developers" is designed for software professionals, system administrators, DevOps engineers, and cloud architects who aim to master Infrastructure as Code (IaC) using Terraform. Basic knowledge of cloud computing and some experience with coding will aid in comprehending the book's content.

## Codes Usage

Are you in need of some helpful code examples to assist you in your programming and documentation? Look no further! Our book offers a wealth of supplemental material, including code examples and exercises.

Not only is this book here to aid you in getting your job done, but you have our permission to use the example code in your programs and documentation. However, please note that if you are reproducing a significant portion of the code, we do require you to contact us for permission.

But don't worry, using several chunks of code from this book in your program or answering a question by citing our book and quoting example code does not require permission. But if you do choose to give credit, an attribution typically includes the title, author, publisher, and ISBN. For example, "Terraform for Developers by Kimiko Lee".

If you are unsure whether your intended use of the code examples falls under fair use or the permissions outlined above, please do not hesitate to reach out to us at support@gitforgits.com.

We are happy to assist and clarify any concerns.

# Acknowledgement

I owe a tremendous debt of gratitude to GitforGits, for their unflagging enthusiasm and wise counsel throughout the entire process of writing this book. Their knowledge and careful editing helped make sure the piece was useful for people of all reading levels and comprehension skills. In addition, I'd like to thank everyone involved in the publishing process for their efforts in making this book a reality. Their efforts, from copyediting to advertising, made the project what it is today.

Finally, I'd like to express my gratitude to everyone who has shown me unconditional love and encouragement throughout my life. Their support was crucial to the completion of this book. I appreciate your help with this endeavour and your continued interest in my career.

# CHAPTER 1: INTRODUCTION TO TERRAFORM AND INFRASTRUCTURE AS CODE (IaC)

# Introduction to Terraform and IaC

## Overview

In the realm of software development and system administration, the introduction of Infrastructure as Code (IaC) marked a significant evolution. Before delving into the specifics of Terraform, it is crucial to understand what Infrastructure as Code means, how it has evolved over time, and why it has become such a vital aspect of modern DevOps practices.

In traditional IT setups, system administrators manually managed the servers and other infrastructure components. This process was error-prone and inconsistent, often resulting in the dreaded "it works on my machine" scenario. Additionally, scaling the infrastructure in response to growing user demands was a time-consuming and complex task.

## Emergence of IaC

IaC emerged as a response to these challenges, bringing in principles from software development into system administration. Just as source code defines the behavior of an application, Infrastructure as Code is a model where IT infrastructure is defined and managed using code. This approach allows developers and system administrators to automate the process of provisioning and managing servers, databases, networks, and other infrastructure components.

IaC tools allow infrastructure setup to be automated, consistent, and repeatable. Developers can write scripts in a high-level language, which the IaC tool can then interpret to set up the infrastructure. This code can be version controlled, shared, and reviewed just like any other software codebase. If the infrastructure needs to be scaled up or down, or if there's a need to replicate the setup, the code can simply be run again with the necessary parameters.

IaC has its roots in server configuration tools like Puppet, Chef, and Ansible, which automated the process of configuring servers. These tools marked the initial wave of IaC, focusing on mutable infrastructure—where existing servers were updated and reconfigured in place. However, these tools often ran into problems with drift, where the actual state of a server diverged from the desired state defined in code, leading to inconsistencies and failures.

This led to the evolution of the next wave of IaC tools like Terraform, AWS CloudFormation, and Google Cloud Deployment Manager. These tools embraced the concept of immutable infrastructure, where servers and other resources are not updated in place. Instead, if a change is required, the existing resources are destroyed, and new ones are created based on the code definitions. This approach reduces the risk of drift and provides more consistent and reliable deployments.

## Arrival of Terraform

Terraform, an open-source tool developed by HashiCorp, has emerged as one of the leading IaC tools in this second wave. Terraform allows you to define and provide data center infrastructure using a declarative configuration language. This language is both human-readable and machine-interactive, making it easy to use, learn, and integrate into the existing workflows.

The main advantages of Terraform lie in its platform-agnostic approach and extensibility. It supports a multitude of providers, from on-premises solutions like VMware to a wide variety of cloud services such as AWS, Google Cloud, and Azure, and even SaaS applications. With Terraform, you can manage a diverse set of services with the same workflow, allowing for increased productivity and efficiency.

Terraform is also designed with modularity in mind. It promotes code reuse and shared modules, which can reduce duplication and boost collaboration across teams. Terraform's modularity also makes it a valuable tool for managing microservices architectures, which require the orchestration of numerous small, independent services.

# Advantages and Merits of IaC

The advent of Infrastructure as Code (IaC) has revolutionized the way organizations provision and manage their IT infrastructure. The ability to automate and streamline these processes has brought an array of benefits.

In this context, we will outline the key advantages and merits of IaC.

- Speed and Efficiency: With IaC, tasks that previously took hours or even days to complete can be accomplished in mere minutes. This speed is due to the automated nature of IaC, which enables the simultaneous creation, update, or deletion of multiple infrastructure resources. Consequently, developers can focus more on coding and less on managing the underlying infrastructure.

- Consistency and Reliability: Manual infrastructure management often leads to inconsistencies due to human error. However, IaC eliminates such discrepancies as the infrastructure setup is defined in code and executed by machines. This ensures a reliable and consistent environment, reducing the possibility of discrepancies between development, testing, and production environments.

- Scalability and Flexibility: With IaC, scaling infrastructure is as simple as adjusting a few parameters in a script. Whether you need to cater to an increasing user base, handle high traffic periods, or create duplicate environments for testing, IaC enables you to do so quickly and efficiently. Also, IaC tools can handle various cloud, virtualization, and container technologies, offering flexibility in the choice of infrastructure.

- Collaboration and Transparency: IaC paves the way for better collaboration between development and operations teams. The code that defines the infrastructure serves as a single source of truth. This enables cross-functional teams to understand how the infrastructure is configured, leading to increased transparency and collaboration.

- Version Control and Auditability: Just like application source code, infrastructure code can be version controlled. This provides a historical record of all changes, who made them, and when. Version control also enables rollbacks to previous infrastructure states if an issue arises. Additionally, IaC supports auditability requirements, providing a clear trail of what was changed and when, critical in regulated industries.

- Cost-Effectiveness: IaC helps organizations save costs in various ways. The increased efficiency and speed reduce the time (and hence cost) associated with infrastructure management tasks. Automated scaling helps optimize resource usage and avoid over-provisioning, thereby saving costs. The ability to tear down resources when they're not in use, such as overnight or on weekends, further adds to the savings.

- Risk Mitigation and Recovery: IaC reduces risk by removing manual intervention from the infrastructure management process. Furthermore, because the infrastructure's state is codified, disaster recovery becomes a less daunting prospect. In the event of a critical failure, the infrastructure can be reliably reproduced from the IaC scripts.

- Testing and Validation: IaC enables 'infrastructure testing'. We can validate the infrastructure's behavior under different conditions, ensuring that the systems will perform as expected. This approach allows you to catch and correct potential issues before they affect the production environment.

- Immutable Infrastructure: IaC enables the creation of immutable infrastructure, where updates and changes are made by replacing resources rather than modifying them in place. This approach significantly reduces the chances of configuration drift, leading to more stable and reliable systems.

- Self-Documenting: The code used in IaC inherently documents the infrastructure setup. It clearly defines what resources are needed and how they are configured, reducing the need for separate documentation. This aspect also simplifies the onboarding process for new team members, who can understand the infrastructure setup by examining the code.

- Future-Proofing: IaC is a key enabler of modern IT practices such as DevOps, CI/CD (Continuous Integration/Continuous Deployment), and microservices. Adopting IaC helps future-proof the infrastructure management practices, ensuring that the organization can leverage these practices to stay competitive in the ever-evolving technology landscape.

- Environment Parity: With IaC, you can mirror the production environment in development, testing, and staging with minimal effort. This environment parity reduces bugs and outages caused by differences in environments, making the software delivery process more efficient.

By adopting IaC, businesses can manage their infrastructure with the same precision, repeatability, and consistency as their application code. This evolution is vital in a world where IT infrastructure is becoming increasingly complex and dynamic. It minimizes the chance for human error, enhances speed, promotes cost efficiency, and provides a platform for scalability.

# Elements of Infrastructure as Code

Infrastructure as Code (IaC) represents an innovative approach to managing IT infrastructure. To understand how it works, it is crucial to comprehend its core components and their functions. The main elements of IaC include Ad Hoc Scripting tools, Server Templating tools, Configuration Management tools, Orchestration tools, and Provisioning tools. Let us take a detailed look at each of these elements.

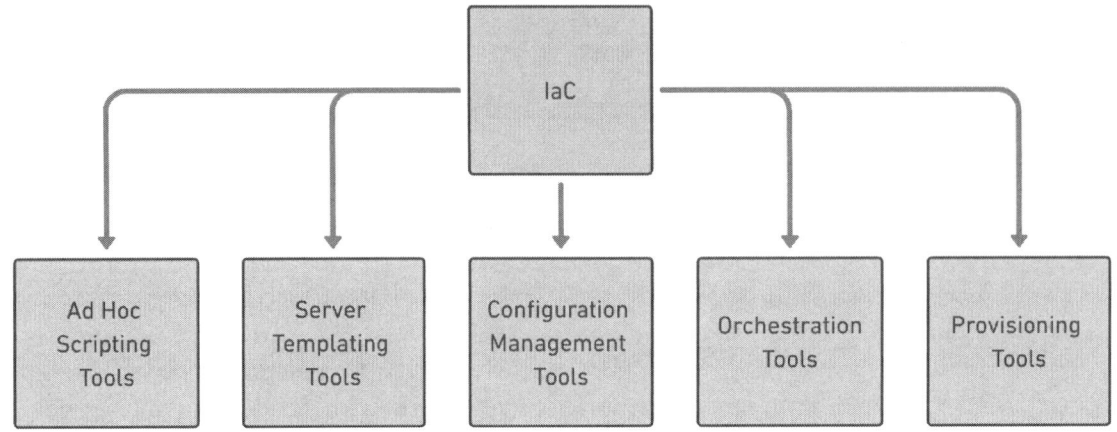

**Fig.1.1 Key Components of Infrastructure as Code**

# Ad Hoc Scripting Tools

Ad hoc scripting represents the foundational level of IaC. It involves creating scripts for automating repetitive tasks, such as installing packages, configuring settings, or managing users. While this approach provides some automation benefits, it also poses several challenges. Scripts may be specific to a certain operating system or environment, leading to portability issues. They also require manual execution and do not inherently support idempotency, meaning running the same script multiple times may produce different outcomes. Despite these limitations, ad hoc scripting remains a common entry point for organizations starting their IaC journey.

# Server Templating Tools

Server templates offer a higher level of abstraction for defining server configurations. They capture the desired state of a server's configuration, including the operating system, installed packages, and system settings. Tools like Packer, Docker, and Vagrant allow users to define server templates in code and build consistent, repeatable server images. These images can then be deployed across various environments, whether on-premises or in the cloud. Server templating is a significant improvement over ad hoc scripting, providing more consistency and repeatability. However, it still leaves certain aspects of infrastructure management unaddressed, such as managing dependencies between servers or maintaining the desired state over time.

# Configuration Management Tools

Configuration Management tools like Puppet, Chef, Ansible, and SaltStack provide a more holistic approach to infrastructure management. They allow you to define the desired state of the entire infrastructure, not just individual servers, in code. These tools maintain the defined state over time, applying changes as needed to keep the actual state in sync with the desired state. They also handle dependencies between different components of the infrastructure. For example, they can ensure that a database server is up and running before deploying an application that relies on it. Configuration management tools typically use a declarative language, allowing you to specify what you want the infrastructure to look like without having to detail how to get there.

# Orchestration Tools

Orchestration tools like Kubernetes, Docker Swarm, and Apache Mesos focus on managing application deployments in containerized environments. They handle tasks such as scheduling containers on available resources, maintaining their desired state (e.g., the number of container instances), and managing communication between containers. Orchestration tools complement IaC by allowing for efficient, reliable, and scalable deployment of applications on the infrastructure provisioned by IaC tools.

# Provisioning Tools

Provisioning tools, such as Terraform, AWS CloudFormation, and Google Cloud Deployment Manager, enable users to define and manage infrastructure resources like networks, load balancers, databases, and virtual machines in a consistent and repeatable manner. These tools extend the concept of IaC beyond the configuration of individual servers to the management of the broader infrastructure landscape. The main advantage of provisioning tools like Terraform is their cloud-agnostic nature. They allow for managing resources across multiple cloud platforms using a single unified language and workflow. Additionally, they support a declarative approach, where you specify the desired state of the infrastructure and the tool figures out how to achieve it. Provisioning tools also maintain state information, tracking the current state of the resources and using it to determine what changes need to be applied to reach the desired state.

Each of these elements plays a unique role in the broader IaC landscape. They all contribute to the main goal of IaC: creating a consistent, repeatable, and automated approach to managing IT infrastructure. However, the choice of which tools to use depends on the specific needs and the maturity of the IaC practices.

Many organizations start with ad hoc scripting and server templating as they begin their IaC journey. As their needs grow, they may incorporate configuration management tools to handle more complex scenarios and maintain their infrastructure's desired state over time. Container-based deployments may require the use of orchestration tools, while multi-cloud environments could benefit from the use of cloud-agnostic provisioning tools like

Terraform.

# Core Principles of Terraform

Terraform, created by HashiCorp, is a popular Infrastructure as Code (IaC) tool that allows users to define and provide data center infrastructure using a declarative configuration language. It has emerged as a key player in the DevOps world due to its flexibility, simplicity, and wide support for different cloud providers. To comprehend how Terraform works and to use it effectively, it's essential to understand the core principles upon which it operates.

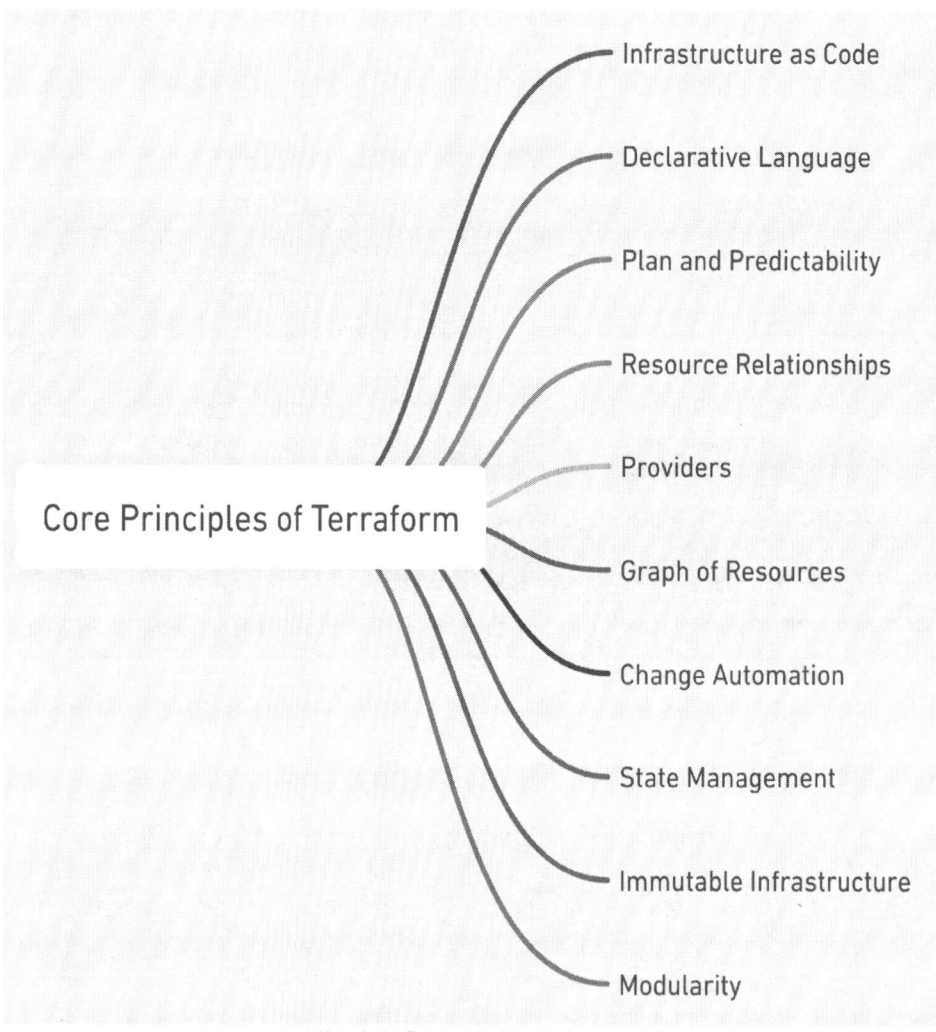

**Fig 1.2 Core Principles of Terraform**

Infrastructure as Code: Terraform uses a high-level syntax to describe infrastructure, allowing you to codify APIs into declarative configuration files. These files can be shared amongst team members, treated as code, edited, reviewed, and version controlled. By doing so, Terraform makes the infrastructure deployment process repeatable with minimal human intervention, reducing the likelihood of human errors and discrepancies between environments.

Declarative Language: Terraform uses a declarative language, HashiCorp Configuration Language (HCL), allowing users to define what the infrastructure should look like. We declare resources, and Terraform carries out the actions needed to reach the desired state. This differs from an imperative approach where one needs to specify how to achieve the desired state. The advantage of a declarative model is that it abstracts the underlying details of infrastructure management, making the code more readable and scalable.

Plan and Predictability: A unique feature of Terraform is the ability to generate an execution plan detailing what it will do to reach the desired state. This plan provides a preview of the changes that will be made, enhancing predictability and control. Once the plan is reviewed and confirmed, Terraform implements the proposed actions, ensuring that the infrastructure aligns with the code.

Resource Relationships: Terraform understands and manages dependencies between resources, enabling the creation of complex infrastructures. Users specify relationships in the code, and Terraform ensures resources are created, updated, or deleted in the proper order. This automated management of dependencies simplifies the orchestration of multi-layer architectures and enhances efficiency.

Providers: Terraform uses a plugin-based architecture with providers to interact with different cloud and infrastructure services. Providers extend Terraform's functionality, allowing it to manage a broad range of resources such as public cloud (AWS, GCP, Azure), private cloud (VMWare), database technologies (MySQL, PostgreSQL), and many more. This wide-ranging support makes Terraform versatile and cloud-agnostic.

Graph of Resources: Internally, Terraform builds a graph of all the resources, and parallelizes the creation and modification of any non-dependent resources. This results in efficient provisioning of infrastructure.

Change Automation: With its built-in planning and applying functionalities, Terraform automates changes to infrastructure. It compares the current state of the infrastructure with the desired state defined in the code and generates a plan for reaching the desired state. Terraform then executes this plan, updating the infrastructure as needed. This approach minimizes manual intervention, thereby reducing errors and boosting efficiency.

State Management: Terraform maintains a state file that maps resources to the configuration, keeps track of metadata, and improves performance for large infrastructures. It uses this state to create plans and make changes to the infrastructure. State can be stored locally or remotely, and can be shared among team members for collaborative work.

Immutable Infrastructure: Terraform supports the principle of immutable infrastructure, which reduces inconsistencies in environments and makes deployments more reliable. Instead of updating existing infrastructure, Terraform provisions a new set of resources alongside the old ones, and once the new infrastructure is verified, the old resources are destroyed.

Modularity: Terraform supports modularity with "modules," which are containers for multiple resources that are used together. Modules can be reused across the infrastructure, which helps in managing common configurations and reduces repetition and complexity.

# Architecture of Terraform

Understanding the architecture of Terraform is crucial to leveraging its capabilities fully. The architecture comprises several key components that interact seamlessly to deliver an efficient, repeatable, and consistent infrastructure management solution.

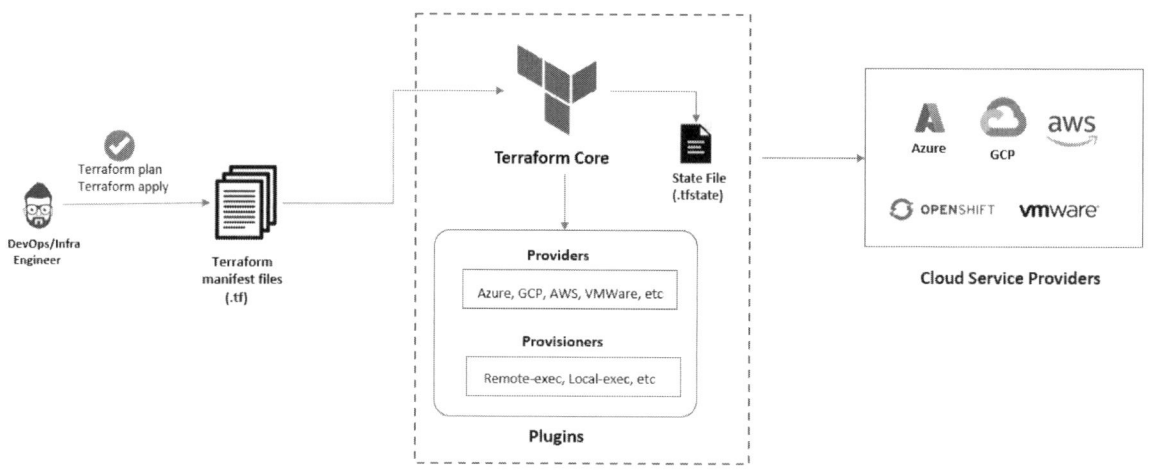

**Fig 1.3 Terraform Architecture**

*Source: https://spacelift.io/blog/terraform-architecture*

Core and Plugins: Terraform follows a plugin-based architecture. The core is written in Go and interacts with a variety of plugins to provide its functionality. These plugins are binaries that the core executes. The core handles resource lifecycle, state storage, and the construction of the resource graph, while the plugins provide a way for the core to interact with different platforms and services.

Providers and Provisioners: Plugins come in two primary forms: Providers and Provisioners. Providers are plugins that Terraform uses to interact with remote systems. They are responsible for understanding API interactions and exposing resources. They encapsulate a set of resource APIs, providing an interface for the core to manage these resources on the target platform. Examples include AWS, Azure, GCP, and many others.

Provisioners, on the other hand, are a kind of plugin that is used to execute scripts on a local or remote machine as part of resource creation or destruction. Provisioners can be used for bootstrapping a resource, preparing it for use, or cleaning up a resource just before its destruction. However, as a rule of thumb, it's best to use provisioners as a last resort; prefer to use the appropriate provider to manage the desired state of the resources.

Terraform Configurations: Terraform configurations are the main point of interaction for users. They are written in HashiCorp Configuration Language (HCL) and define what the infrastructure should look like. The configurations define resources and their dependencies, and Terraform uses this to create a dependency graph which it then traverses to create, modify, or destroy resources.

Terraform CLI (Command Line Interface): The Terraform CLI is the primary way users interact with Terraform. It provides commands for deploying and managing infrastructure as per the configurations. The CLI interprets the configurations and makes the necessary calls to providers or provisioners, handles state, and updates the user about the status of the operations.

State: The state is a JSON-formatted file that Terraform generates to track the infrastructure it manages. It uses this to map resources in the configuration to real-world objects in the infrastructure provider and to store metadata. The state is crucial as it enables Terraform to identify what it needs to do to bring the infrastructure in line with the configurations. It allows Terraform to perform efficient updates and prevent duplicate resources.

Backend: The backend in Terraform is a location where the state file is stored and is used to execute operations. Backends can be local (on the file system) or remote (like S3, HTTP, Artifactory, etc.). Remote backends enable state sharing for team collaboration, can keep a historical state of the infrastructure, and can run operations in the backend itself.

Resource Graph: Terraform builds a graph of all the resources, and parallelizes the creation and modification of any non-dependent resources, optimizing the provisioning process. The graph also helps Terraform understand and respect dependencies.

Workspace: A workspace is a concept that Terraform uses to manage different environments (like development, staging, production). Each workspace has a separate state file, making it possible to deploy similar infrastructure with the same code but with different variables.

Modules: Modules in Terraform are self-contained packages of Terraform configurations that are managed as a group. Modules can be used across multiple environments, increasing reusability and maintainability.

Terraform's architecture is, in short, purposefully made to be easy to understand while also being highly adaptable and powerful. Users who have a thorough understanding of its architecture are better able to make full use of its capabilities for managing infrastructure. This enables more efficient provisioning and management, as well as a better understanding of how changes will affect the infrastructure, which ultimately results in increased safety and predictability.

# Features of Terraform

Following the discussion of the core principles and architecture of Terraform, it is also important to highlight the various features that make Terraform an industry-standard tool for managing infrastructure as code.

- Platform Agnostic: Perhaps one of the most significant features of Terraform is its platform-agnostic nature. Terraform's use of providers allows it to interface with a wide variety of platforms, ranging from major cloud providers like AWS, Azure, and Google Cloud, to smaller, specialized services. This ability to work with different platforms allows organizations to manage a multi-cloud strategy efficiently, offering a unified method to interact with diverse cloud ecosystems.

- Declarative Syntax: Terraform uses the declarative HashiCorp Configuration Language (HCL). In this model, you describe the desired state of the infrastructure, and Terraform figures out how to achieve that state. This approach eliminates the need for operators to write detailed step-by-step instructions, making the code more readable and maintainable.

- Planning and Preview of Changes: The terraform plan command is a powerful feature that provides a preview of what changes Terraform will apply before it actually executes them. This feature allows users to catch and prevent potentially destructive actions, increasing the predictability and safety of managing infrastructure changes.

- Resource Graph: Terraform creates a graph of all resources and understands their dependencies. This graph is used during the planning phase to parallelize the creation and modification of resources, and it is also used during the apply phase to ensure that resources are created in the correct order.

- Modularity and Reusability with Modules: Terraform encourages code reuse through the use of modules. A module is a container for multiple resources that are used together and can be used across different projects, thereby promoting the DRY (Don't Repeat Yourself) principle.

- Immutable and Versioned Infrastructure: Terraform treats infrastructure changes as incremental versions, much like a version control system does for code. When you want to make changes, Terraform calculates the difference between the current state and the desired state and applies the changes, essentially creating a new version of the infrastructure. This approach encourages the principle of Immutable Infrastructure, where infrastructure is never modified after it's deployed. If changes are required, new infrastructure is provisioned to replace the old one.

- Supports State Backends: Terraform allows storing state information in various backends like local filesystems or remote data stores such as HashiCorp's Consul, AWS S3, Google Cloud Storage, etc. This allows for advanced state management, facilitates team collaboration, and enables versioning and backup.

- Workspace Management: Terraform supports the concept of workspaces, allowing you to manage multiple environments (like development, staging, and production) with the same configuration but different state files. This feature helps to segregate and manage different deployment environments effectively.

- Collaboration and Sharing: Terraform provides features to share and collaborate on infrastructure configuration. Terraform Cloud and Enterprise offer collaboration for teams, with features like remote state management, private module registry, and policy as code.

- Detailed Documentation: Terraform provides comprehensive and robust documentation that includes a registry of public modules and providers. The detailed documentation aids in understanding how to use the tool and encourages best practices.

- Extensible: Terraform is designed to be extensible with plugins. The plugin system allows the community to build support for new providers and provisioners, making it adaptable to emerging technologies and platforms.

To sum up, these features make Terraform an effective and efficient tool for managing complex, multi-provider infrastructure. Terraform's power lies not just in its ability to manage infrastructure resources but also in the way it enables teams to treat infrastructure management as a coding practice, thereby enhancing team collaboration, promoting best practices, and ultimately leading to more reliable and predictable infrastructure management.

# Summary

In this chapter, we began exploring the topic of Infrastructure as Code (IaC), gaining an understanding of its history as well as the benefits it brings to modern software development. We went over how IaC imitates software development practices for infrastructure management, offering benefits such as code review, version control, and continuous integration and delivery. The components of IaC, such as ad-hoc scripting, server templating, configuration management, orchestration, and provisioning, were dissected in order to gain a better understanding of how these components work together to make infrastructure management more effective.

After that, we dove deeper into the intricacies of Terraform, which is considered to be one of the most powerful IaC tools. We investigated its fundamental principles, which included its declarative language, its plan and predictability, its resource relationships, its providers, its state management, and its modularity. We placed a strong emphasis on the concept of declaring what resources we require and allowing Terraform to figure out how to fulfil those requirements. This is a strategy that abstracts the underlying details, which makes the code more readable and scalable. This also encompasses the power of planning changes before putting them into action, which results in increased predictability and control over changes.

Following that, we did some research on the architecture and features of Terraform. The lifecycle of resources is managed by the core, and plugins, such as providers and provisioners, extend Terraform's functionality to manage a wide variety of resources. The architecture is centered on the core and plugins, and the core manages the lifecycle of resources. Terraform is an effective and efficient tool for managing complex infrastructure composed of multiple providers because of its features. These features include its platform-agnostic nature, declarative syntax, preview of changes, resource graph, modularity with modules, support for state backends, and workspace management. Extensibility, collaboration options, and extensive documentation are just a few of the features that further enhance Terraform's utility in managing infrastructure as code.

# CHAPTER 2: GETTING STARTED WITH TERRAFORM

# Installing and Setting up Terraform

In Chapter 1, we did familiarize ourselves with the fundamentals of Infrastructure as Code (IaC) and delved deep into the principles, architecture, and features of Terraform, a leading tool in the IaC landscape. We discovered the power of using declarative language for managing infrastructure, the efficiency of planning and predictability in handling changes, and the importance of state in maintaining consistency and avoiding conflicts. Now, we're ready to roll up our sleeves and get our hands dirty with Terraform.

Let us begin with the installation of Terraform on a Linux-based system. As of this writing, the latest version of Terraform is Terraform 0.15.3. Please note that Terraform versions are regularly updated; always check the official Terraform website for the latest version.

## Download Appropriate Package

Open a terminal and use wget to download the package. Replace the URL with the link to the latest version found on the official Terraform downloads page.

```
wget
https://releases.hashicorp.com/terraform/0.15.3/terraform_0.15.3_linux_amd64.zip
```

## Extract Package

Next, you'll need to extract the downloaded zip file. This will contain the binary 'terraform'. We'll use unzip to extract it.

```
unzip terraform_0.15.3_linux_amd64.zip
```

## Move Binary to PATH Location

To make the terraform command conveniently available from any location in the terminal, move the 'terraform' binary to a directory that is in the PATH. A common choice is the /usr/local/bin directory.

```
sudo mv terraform /usr/local/bin/
```

## Verify Installation

Finally, you can verify that the installation was successful by checking the version of

Terraform.

```
terraform version
```

If the installation is successful, this command will output the version of Terraform that you installed, like so:

```
Terraform v0.15.3
```

We can now say that Terraform is up and running on the Linux machine. We are now prepared to begin defining, deploying, and modifying infrastructure in a manner that is both secure and effective. Keep in mind that the Terraform journey is a marathon, not a sprint, and that subsequent chapters will cover more advanced aspects of this powerful tool that we will be exploring.

# Setting up Microsoft Azure Account

Let us move forward with establishing the Microsoft Azure account, shall we? Microsoft's Azure is a cloud computing service, and for the next year, users can take advantage of Microsoft's generous offer of a free account. In addition to this, there are some services that will always be provided at no cost. Because of this incredible offer, you won't have to worry about paying any money up front to investigate and become accustomed to the platform. Now that we've established that, let me walk you through the process of setting up the account step by step. Keep in mind that the goal is to acquaint you with all of Azure's features and services so that you feel confident using them.

## Sign up Azure Free Account

Visit the Azure Free Account page here and click on the "Start free" button. If you already have a Microsoft account, you can sign in, otherwise you will need to create one.

## Verify Identity

During the sign-up process, you will be asked to verify the identity. This requires a valid phone number and a credit card. Don't worry, as long as you manage the services and don't go over the free usage limits, you won't be charged. This information is required to verify identity and prevent fraudulent use.

## Choose Subscription

Choose "Free Trial" for the subscription unless you have a specific need for a different subscription. This will grant you access to free services for 12 months, $200 credit for the first 30 days, and over 25 services that are always free.

## Set up Account

Fill out the account setup form with the details. We will need to provide the name, email address, country, and other information. We will also need to agree to the terms and conditions.

## Confirmation

After a few moments, you should receive a confirmation that the account setup is complete. We can now start exploring Azure services!

## Navigate to Azure Portal

Once the account is set up, you can access all the Azure services from the Azure portal. We can visit the Azure portal here.

Following the configuration of the Azure account, we will now move on to configuring Azure for Terraform. However, before we continue, it is highly recommended that you become acquainted with the Azure portal, as well as its many services and the locations of those services. Keep in mind that the greater the power, the greater the responsibility. When you are finished using a resource, you should make sure to disable or delete it so that you are not charged for it.

# Create Azure Service for Terraform

Once the Azure account is set up, you'll need to create a Service Principal in Azure, which is an application in the Azure Active Directory (AD) that will have permissions to manage resources in the Azure subscription. Terraform will use this service principal to create, manage, and delete resources in the Azure account.

## Install Azure CLI

Azure CLI (Command-Line Interface) is a command-line tool for managing Azure resources. We can install it on macOS, Linux, and Windows and run it in the terminal. Visit Install the Azure CLI for detailed installation instructions.

## Login Azure CLI

Open a terminal and run the following command to log in. We will be prompted to open a URL in the web browser and enter a code.

```
az login
```

Follow the instructions to authenticate.

## Create Service Principal

Once authenticated, create a Service Principal with the az ad sp create-for-rbac command.

```
az ad sp create-for-rbac --role="Contributor" --
scopes="/subscriptions/YOUR_SUBSCRIPTION_ID"
```
Replace "YOUR_SUBSCRIPTION_ID" with the actual Azure subscription ID. We can find the subscription ID in the Azure portal under "Subscriptions".

This command will output five values:
appId: This is the client_id defined above.
displayName: This is the name of the application.
name: This is the fully qualified URL of the application.
password: This is the client_secret defined above.
tenant: This is the tenant_id defined above.

Keep these values safe in a separate location. In order to authenticate to Azure, they will be used in the configuration of the Terraform project. After configuring the Azure Service Principal, you are now able to use Terraform in conjunction with Azure. After discussing how to set up the Terraform configuration for Azure in the following section, we will move on to beginning the management of resources.

# Configure Terraform for Azure

With an Azure service principal created, we can now configure Terraform to authenticate with Azure and provision resources.

The next step is to create a Terraform configuration file that will specify the Azure provider settings and define the infrastructure components to deploy. Within the provider block, we need to reference the credentials gathered from creating the service principal - the subscription ID, client ID, client secret, and tenant ID. This allows Terraform to authenticate securely using the service principal without needing manual login.

The Azure resources to deploy, such as virtual machines, networks, storage, and databases, are defined in the resources section. Here we can build out the complete infrastructure architecture in code using Terraform's Azure resource types. The flexibility of Terraform allows infrastructure to be coded from the ground up. We can start from basic networking components like virtual networks and subnets, build up to virtual machines, then layer on additional services. Once the configuration file is defined with the provider settings and resource specifications, we can initialize the working directory, run a plan to verify the changes, and apply the changes to deploy the Azure resources.

Following is a sample program to perform the successful configuration of Terraform and begin using it for resource provisioning:

# Create Directory and Configuration File

Create a new directory where you'll store the Terraform configuration files. We can do this via the terminal:

```
mkdir terraform-azure
cd terraform-azure
```

Then, within this directory, create a new file called main.tf. This will be the main Terraform configuration file.

```
touch main.tf
```

# Define Terraform Azure Provider

Open the main.tf file in the preferred text editor and start by specifying the Terraform Azure provider. The Azure provider is used to interact with the many resources supported by Azure. The provider needs to be configured with a subscription ID, client ID, client secret, and tenant ID.

Replace the placeholders in the following code with the respective Azure Service Principal credentials:

```
provider "azurerm" {
  features = {}
  subscription_id = "the-subscription-id"
  client_id      = "the-client-id"
  client_secret  = "the-client-secret"
  tenant_id      = "the-tenant-id"
}
```

# Initialize Terraform

Once you've saved the main.tf file, go back to the terminal and make sure you're in the terraform-azure directory. Run the terraform init command, which will initialize the directory and download the Azure provider.

```
terraform init
```

If the main.tf file is correctly configured with the Azure Service Principal, you should see a message indicating that the "Terraform has been successfully initialized!"

# Define Infrastructure

Now you're ready to define some infrastructure. Let us start small by creating a resource group. Add the following code to the main.tf file:

```
resource "azurerm_resource_group" "rg" {
  name     = "myResourceGroup"
  location = "West US"
}
```

This code tells Terraform to create a resource group named "myResourceGroup" in the "West US" region.

# Plan and Apply

After defining the desired infrastructure architecture in Terraform configuration files, the next step is to run terraform plan. This constructs an execution plan that previews the changes that will be made to reach the desired state.

The plan command compares the current state snapshot saved in the Terraform state file against the new configuration code. It then calculates the create, update, and destroy actions needed to reconcile the actual and expected infrastructure.

```
terraform plan
```

If everything looks good, apply the changes:

```
terraform apply
```

After confirming, Terraform will reach out to Azure and create the resource group.

So, now that's excellent work you have achieved. Provisioning infrastructure on Azure using Terraform is a major accomplishment. We have hands-on experience under the belt and a foundation to build upon. In the chapters ahead, we will explore more advanced Terraform capabilities to help manage even greater infrastructure complexity.

# Terraform Commands In-use

Terraform provides a set of commands that perform different actions on our infrastructure code and configurations. The most common commands are used for core operations like initializing, planning, applying and destroying changes.

To illustrate these commands, let us assume we have a simple Terraform configuration file called main.tf. This config sets up the Azure provider and defines a single Azure resource group to create. With this main.tf file, we can walk through the typical workflow and usage of key Terraform commands:

## terraform init

This command is used to initialize a working directory containing Terraform configuration files. It's the first command that should be run after writing a new Terraform configuration.

```
terraform init
```

Upon execution, it downloads the required provider plugins, sets up the backend for storing the state file, and performs some initial validations.

# terraform validate

This command checks the validity of the Terraform files in the directory. It checks for syntax errors, attribute names, and value types. It doesn't check whether resources exist or not.

```
terraform validate
```

If the configuration is valid, the command will output "Success! The configuration is valid."

# terraform fmt

This command is used to rewrite Terraform files to a canonical format and style. It helps in maintaining consistent coding practices and improves the readability of the Terraform code.

```
terraform fmt
```

After running this command, you'll notice that the Terraform files have been updated to have a consistent style.

# terraform plan

This command creates an execution plan. It determines what actions are necessary to achieve the desired state defined in the configuration files. It's a good practice to run this command before applying changes, as it allows you to preview the changes that will be made.

```
terraform plan
```

This will output a detailed plan of the resources that will be created, modified, or destroyed.

# terraform apply

This command applies the desired changes to reach the desired state of the configuration, or the pre-determined set of actions generated by a terraform plan execution plan.

```
terraform apply
```

This will output a plan and prompt you to confirm that you want to proceed with the changes. Once confirmed, it will create, modify, or destroy resources as defined in the plan.

## terraform show

This command is used to provide human-readable output from a state or plan file.

```
terraform show
```

It will print out the current state of the resources.

## terraform destroy

This command destroys the Terraform-managed infrastructure.

```
terraform destroy
```

Similar to terraform apply, this command will prompt you to confirm that you want to proceed. Once confirmed, it will destroy all the resources defined in the Terraform files.

These are some basic commands to get you started. As you continue working with Terraform, you'll encounter more commands that provide more specific or advanced functionality.

# Terraform CLI

The Terraform CLI (Command Line Interface) is a tool that makes it possible for system administrators and developers to manage infrastructure as code (IaC). This tool is well-organized and straightforward to use. It does this by abstracting the complexities of the API and providing a coherent interface that integrates seamlessly with the industry's leading service providers, such as AWS, Google Cloud, Azure, and a great many others.

## User-Friendly

The Terraform CLI has a user-friendly interface that provides structured, easy-to-follow commands that are intuitive for users, whether they're beginners or experienced professionals. Commands such as init, plan, apply, and destroy are straightforward and self-explanatory, enabling users to quickly get started with managing their infrastructure.

# Extensible

One of Terraform's core features is its extensibility. Terraform uses a plugin-based architecture, and all the providers it supports (like AWS, Azure, GCP, etc.) are implemented as plugins. Terraform CLI manages the lifecycle of these plugins, providing commands to initialize and configure the providers. If the infrastructure service you want to manage is not supported out of the box, you can write the own custom plugin.

# Multi-Platform

A key strength of Terraform CLI is its availability across Linux, Windows, and MacOS operating systems. This wide platform support provides flexibility to users. The same Terraform workflow and interface can be leveraged regardless of the underlying OS. Whether running Terraform from a desktop workstation, cloud shell, or server, the experience remains consistent.

This allows teams to standardize on Terraform for infrastructure automation while using the preferred platforms for various tasks. No matter the OS, the CLI usage stays the same. Cross-platform availability also enables Terraform to be incorporated throughout the infrastructure pipeline. Terraform configs can be authored on a developer's desktop, validated on a Linux CI system, and applied in production on Windows.

# State Management

Terraform CLI centrally manages state - a persistent snapshot of the infrastructure under management. State is used to map real-world resources to configurations. It allows Terraform to determine create, read, update, and delete actions by comparing config to state. This enables detailed execution plans and change automation.

State also caches resource attributes to improve performance at scale. The terraform refresh command updates state from infrastructure sources to sync them. Outside the CLI, operators can inspect state content with terraform show and pull/push state files such as for backup. State data can also be migrated across backends.

# Planning and Predictability

The terraform plan command is one of the powerful features of Terraform CLI. It allows users to see which actions Terraform will perform prior to making any changes, increasing predictability and reducing the chances of unexpected results. Furthermore, it creates an execution plan that describes what it will do to reach the desired state. This plan can be saved and passed to terraform apply command to ensure only the pre-calculated actions are executed.

## Modular and Reusable

One of the most powerful features of Terraform CLI is its support for modules. Modules encapsulate Terraform configurations related to a single infrastructure component and expose them as a cohesive unit with inputs and outputs.

Modules promote reusability of common infrastructure patterns across the codebase. Rather than monolithic configurations, infrastructure can be built compositionally using modular blocks. This reduces duplication and improves maintainability. Modules act as the building blocks for layering infrastructure components. Complex systems can be constructed by combining and connecting modules. With thoughtfully defined interfaces, modules can be shared and reused broadly.

## Workspace Management

Terraform CLI provides workspaces for managing distinct infrastructure environments like development, staging, and production within the same configuration. Workspaces isolate state files, variable values, and backends per environment.

This eliminates unnecessary duplication of configurations while retaining separation of environments. The terraform workspace commands allow seamless switching between workspaces. Environments can share the same source code while being deployed and managed independently.

## Community Support

Terraform benefits from a large open source community building plugins, modules, and tools around the CLI and core project. Community members contribute providers, expanding Terraform's native integrations with new infrastructure platforms and services. They also create and share modules for common patterns.

Beyond code contributions, the community provides education through blogs, talks and documentation. They also offer support via GitHub issues and forum discussions to aid practitioners. This ecosystem of knowledge sharing and support is invaluable for those leveraging Terraform CLI for real-world infrastructure automation.

# HashiCorp Configuration Language (HCL)

HashiCorp Configuration Language (HCL) is the declarative language created specifically for Terraform used to define infrastructure as code. It strikes a balance between being easy for humans to read and write while also being machine-friendly to parse and process.

Some key aspects of HCL:
- Syntax is declarative, describing the desired end-state rather than imperatively

defining steps
- Uses a simple, nested block structure with key-value mappings to define resources
- Supports comments, variables, expressions, functions for additional capabilities
- JSON-compatible so integrates with existing tooling and workflows
- Designed for the infrastructure domain with resource types, providers, provisioners
- Configuration files use .tf extension and can be organized modularly
- HCL is strictly validated and formatted for consistency
- Backward compatible with deprecation cycles to avoid breaking changes

Let us dive into the primary components of the HCL:

# Blocks

The foundational element of HCL syntax is the block. Blocks allow resources, data sources, provider configs and other components to be defined in a declarative, nested structure.

A block has the following anatomy:
- Type - The resource, data source, etc that is being configured.
- Labels - Optional identifiers for the block. This allows targeting the block elsewhere in code.
- Body - Contains arguments, attributes, nested blocks to define the component.

For example:

```
resource "azurerm_resource_group" "rg" {
  name     = "myResourceGroup"
  location = "West US"
}
```

In the above snippet "resource" is the block type, "azurerm_resource_group" is the resource type being instantiated, "rg" is a label that names this block, and the body contains arguments like "name" and "location" to configure the resource.

Blocks can be nested within other blocks to build up configurations compositionally. Arguments and blocks can reference other blocks by label to connect components.

# Arguments

In addition to blocks, HCL configurations also contain arguments. Arguments are used within blocks to assign values to specific configuration settings.

For example, in the azurerm_resource_group block above, "name" and "location" are arguments that set those properties on the resource group:

```
resource "azurerm_resource_group" "rg" {
  name     = "myResourceGroup" // name argument
  location = "West US" // location argument
}
```

The value of an argument can be a literal, variable, expression, or function call. Arguments allow resources to be parameterized and customized without modifying the base configuration block. Changing argument values allows tweaking the component while reusing the overall block definition.

Together with blocks, arguments provide the core syntax constructs that enable operators to define infrastructure resources and architectures declaratively in code using HCL.

## Expressions

Expressions in HCL represent a computed value, either literally or by referencing other objects. Expressions can be used to dynamically generate values for arguments, resource properties, etc.

For example:

```
resource "azurerm_virtual_network" "network" {
  name            = "myVnet"
  address_space   = ["10.0.0.0/16"]
  location        = azurerm_resource_group.rg.location // Expression referencing
rg location
  resource_group_name = azurerm_resource_group.rg.name // Expression from
rg name
}
```

In this snippet, azurerm_resource_group.rg.location and azurerm_resource_group.rg.name are expressions that reference the location and name attributes of the "rg" resource group. The values of those expressions become the arguments for the virtual network's location and resource group name.

Expressions can also apply functions like upper(), lower(), join(), etc to transform values. Complex expressions can combine references, literals, operators, and functions to derive values on the fly. HCL expressions add dynamic capabilities to configs, allowing objects and results of computations to be passed around as parameter values. They are fundamental to creating flexible, DRY infrastructure code.

# Variables and Outputs

Variables allow parameterized values to be passed into Terraform configurations. They are defined using a variable block:

```
variable "instance_size" {
  type = string
}
```

Variables can be set via CLI flags, environment variables, input prompts, and variable definition files. This separates configuration from customization.

Outputs export values from resources in the Terraform state. For example:

```
output "instance_ip" {
  value = aws_instance.server.public_ip
}
```

Now other configurations can reference the instance_ip output. Outputs enable information sharing and simplify usage of Terraform-managed infrastructure.

Together, variables and outputs allow users to:
- Customize infrastructures with different variable values
- Access information about provisioned resources
- Reuse configurations with abstraction between code and customization
- Share data between modules and workspaces

Variables and outputs help make Terraform configurations flexible, self-documenting, and composable. They are key elements of a robust Terraform architecture.

# Functions

Terraform includes a variety of built-in functions that can be used within expressions to transform and combine values.

For example, upper(), lower(), concat(), element(), base64encode() and many more.

Functions enable compute within configs, like formatting strings, merging collections, and calculating math operations. They add flexiblity when deriving dynamic values.

# Modules

Modules encapsulate groups of related resources and allow them to be reused across configurations. A module is defined once then can be instantiated anywhere. Modules have inputs and outputs to customize and access them. They enable abstraction and encapsulation for infrastructure components. Using modules leads to DRY, maintainable code by reducing duplication. New configs can leverage existing modular components.

# Conditionals

Terraform supports conditional logic through ternary conditional expressions:

```
condition ? true_val : false_val
```

The syntax checks a condition and returns one of two values depending on the outcome. This allows element creation and rendering of values to adapt based on variables and conditions in the Terraform codebase.

# Data Structures

HCL supports primitive data structures including strings, lists, maps, objects, and tuples. These allow elements to be grouped and passed around in Terraform code.

For example, a list could represent subnet CIDRs, a map could contain VM-specific settings, an object could hold credential info. Data structures enable complex data manipulation natively within configs. Resources can be parameterized using arrays, maps, etc.

# For Loops

For expressions provide looping capabilities to iterate over data structures like lists and maps.

For example:

```
resource "aws_instance" "server" {
  for_each = toset(["prod", "staging", "dev"])
  # ... instance config
}
```

This would create 3 instances by looping over the provided list of environments. Loops allow resource creation and config to be generated dynamically based on variables.

# Resource Graph

Terraform analyzes dependencies between resources and builds a graph to determine creation order and dependency relationships.

This graph is used to execute changes predictably and efficiently. It enables auto-computed dependencies between resources. Operators can also visualize the graph with terraform graph to understand relationships.

# Local Values

Local values are named expressions that can simplify complex expressions and encourage the reuse of common elements. They are created using the locals block and can be referred throughout the configuration.

```
locals {
  common_tags = {
    Owner = "DevOps Team"
    Service = "Backend"
  }
}


resource "azurerm_resource_group" "rg" {
```

```
name     = "myResourceGroup"
location = "West US"
tags     = local.common_tags
}
```

In the above sample code, a local value common_tags is defined and used as a tag for the Azure resource group.

# Dynamic Blocks

Dynamic blocks allow block content to be generated dynamically based on values in lists, maps, etc.

For example, to create multiple similar resources from a variable list of names:

```
variable "server_names" {
  type = list(string)
}

resource "aws_instance" "server" {
  for_each = var.server_names

  dynamic "ebs_block_device" {
    for_each = var.server_names
    content {
      device_name = "/dev/sda1"
      volume_size = 10
    }
  }
}
```

This would create an ebs_block_device for each instance, keyed by the names in var.server_names. The content of the dynamic block can reference the current element being iterated over in the outer loop.

Dynamic blocks avoid repetitive block definitions and enable programmatic infrastructure generation. They provide flexibility when the number of resources or config details depends on variable input. Dynamic block handling is a powerful HCL construct.

# My First Terraform Configuration

Let us go step by step in creating the first Terraform configuration. We'll create a simple configuration that manages an Azure Resource Group.

## Install Azure CLI

Before we begin, make sure you have the Azure CLI installed if not done as learned in the previous chapter. If you haven't installed it yet, you can follow the instructions in the official Azure CLI documentation: https://docs.microsoft.com/en-us/cli/azure/install-azure-cli

We can log in to the Azure account by using the Azure CLI with the following command:

```
az login
```

Follow the prompts to complete the login process.

## Create Directory for Project

First, you'll need to create a new directory on the system where you'll store the Terraform configuration files. We can do this using the mkdir command:

```
mkdir my_first_terraform_project
cd my_first_terraform_project
```

## Create Terraform Configuration File

Create a new file called main.tf in the project directory. We can use any text editor you like for this.

In main.tf, we will define a resource for an Azure Resource Group. Add the following code:

```
terraform {
  required_providers {
    azurerm = {
```

```
    source  = "hashicorp/azurerm"
    version = "=2.40.0"
   }
  }
}


provider "azurerm" {
  features {}
}


resource "azurerm_resource_group" "my_rg" {
  name     = "myResourceGroup"
  location = "West Europe"
}
```

In this code, we first declare the azurerm provider and specify the version we want to use. Then, we configure the provider by including a provider block with the features attribute set to empty (which is currently required by the Azure provider).

Finally, we define an Azure Resource Group by including a resource block. The block includes a name argument and a location argument. The resource group will be named "myResourceGroup" and will be located in the "West Europe" region.

## Initialize Terraform

Before you can apply the configuration, you need to initialize Terraform. This step downloads the necessary provider plugins. Run the following command:

```
terraform init
```

## Apply Configuration

We are now ready to create the Azure Resource Group. We can do this with the terraform apply command, which will show you a plan and prompt for confirmation:

```
terraform apply
```

With our Terraform configuration authoring complete, the next step is to apply the changes to provision real infrastructure.

We first run terraform plan to verify the planned actions match our intent. The plan shows what resources will be created and config applied. Carefully reviewing the plan output is a critical step before proceeding. We want to ensure no unexpected changes or insecure configurations were introduced inadvertently. If the plan looks good, we can confidently apply it knowing what the outcome will be. Run terraform apply and type yes at the confirmation prompt to go ahead with the apply.

Under the hood, Terraform will execute the pre-determined actions from the plan. It will interact with the Azure provider to create the specified resource group. Outputs will show the progress of resource creation. Terraform handles all API interactions to provision the infrastructure defined in the configuration. Once the apply completes successfully, our Azure resource group has been created! We can inspect its attributes in state using terraform show. The infrastructure now exists in the real world, tracked by the Terraform state file, and matches what we authored in config. This demonstrates the power of infrastructure as code to make changes predictable and reliable.

With a simple plan and apply, we've automated the provisioning of infrastructure safely using Terraform. This represents the first step in a journey toward strengthening the infrastructure as code practices.

# Executing Terraform Configuration

Now that we have authored our first Terraform configuration, the next step is to apply those changes to provision real infrastructure. Applying a Terraform configuration executes the set of actions defined in the code to create, update, or destroy resources. It is the process of reconciling the specified desired state with the actual state.

## Initialize Terraform

Before applying the configuration, you first need to initialize Terraform. This step downloads the Azure provider plugin, sets up the backend for storing the state, and performs a few other necessary tasks. In the terminal, navigate to the directory containing the main.tf file and run:

```
terraform init
```

We should see a message indicating that Terraform has been successfully initialized and that the azurerm provider (the Azure provider for Terraform) has been installed.

## Validate and Format Configuration

Before applying the configuration, it's a good idea to validate and format it to catch any errors and improve readability:

To validate the configuration, run:

```
terraform validate
```

To automatically format the configuration to follow the canonical style, run:

```
terraform fmt
```

## Create Execution Plan

With validation and formatting complete, you can create an execution plan with the terraform plan command:

```
terraform plan
```

This command shows you what actions Terraform will take to apply the configuration, which is very useful for reviewing changes before applying them. The command outputs a detailed plan of the resources that Terraform will create, modify, or destroy.

## Apply Configuration

To apply the configuration and actually create the resources, run:

```
terraform apply
```

Upon running terraform apply, Terraform will again print the execution plan and then prompt you to confirm that you want to proceed. Type yes and hit enter. Terraform will now reach out to Azure and create the Resource Group as defined in the configuration. When it's done, it will print an output showing the resources it created.

With this, you've successfully applied the Terraform configuration. The Resource Group is now being managed by Terraform. If you navigate to the Azure portal, you should be able to see the new Resource Group.

It is important to keep in mind that the ids and properties of the resources that Terraform manages are saved in a file called terraform.tfstate. This file is required for Terraform in order for it to maintain its resource tracking. When you run the terraform apply command, it will automatically create and update itself. Utilizing the terraform destroy command will allow you to get rid of the resources once you have finished using them. It will get rid of any resources that have been generated by Terraform.

# Destroy Resources with Terraform

Being able to cleanly destroy and remove resources with Terraform is just as important as creating them. This capability is especially useful for temporary test or dev environments that need to be easily torn down.

The terraform destroy command is used to destroy all the resources being managed by the current Terraform configuration. It essentially reverses the terraform apply by removing what was created. Terraform will present a destroy plan showing all resources that will be destroyed. This should be carefully reviewed before confirming the destruction just like the apply plan. Once confirmed, Terraform will interact with providers and delete all provisioned infrastructure components tracked in state. Outputs will show the destruction progress.

After a successful terraform destroy, the resources no longer exist in the real-world infrastructure or in state. The environment is back to a clean slate.

Below is the cycle of how to do it:

## Verify the Current State

Before you destroy anything, it can be useful to first check what Terraform is currently managing. We can use the terraform show command for this:

```
terraform show
```

This command will give you a readout of the current state as Terraform sees it.

## Plan the Destruction

While not required, it can be beneficial to see what terraform destroy would do before it does it. To see a plan of what will be destroyed, you can use the terraform plan -destroy command:

```
terraform plan -destroy
```

This will show you a plan with all the resources that are currently managed by Terraform marked for destruction.

## Destroy the Resources

Once you are ready to destroy the resources, run the terraform destroy command:

```
terraform destroy
```

Terraform will show you a plan for what it is going to destroy and ask for confirmation. If everything looks correct, type yes and hit enter. Terraform will then reach out to Azure and destroy the Resource Group. Do not forget that destruction of resources is final and not easily reversible and you shall be absolutely certain to destroy resources before confirming the operation.

After running this command, the resources that were managed by Terraform are now removed. If you run terraform show again, it should report that it is not managing any resources. The cycle of creating, changing, and destroying resources is a fundamental part of working with Terraform and Infrastructure as Code.

# Resource Dependencies

The Terraform tool allows you to create, manage, and connect resources from different service providers, and even different aspects of the same provider. However, to make the best use of these capabilities, it's important to understand how Terraform manages the relationships between resources: these are known as "Resource Dependencies". Resource dependencies in Terraform determine the order in which resources are created, updated, and destroyed. A resource depends on another if its configuration includes a reference to the other's attributes.

For instance, suppose we want to create a virtual network within our resource group in Azure. The creation of the virtual network depends on the resource group being created first because you can't create a virtual network before the resource group it belongs to exists.

Let us add a azurerm_virtual_network to our existing main.tf configuration file:

```
resource "azurerm_virtual_network" "my_vnet" {
  name               = "myVNet"
  address_space      = ["10.0.0.0/16"]
  location           = azurerm_resource_group.my_rg.location
  resource_group_name = azurerm_resource_group.my_rg.name
}
```

In the above sample code, the azurerm_virtual_network resource has an implicit dependency on the azurerm_resource_group resource. This is because the location and resource_group_name attributes of the virtual network resource refer to the azurerm_resource_group.my_rg.name and azurerm_resource_group.my_rg.location attributes.

When you run terraform apply, Terraform constructs a dependency graph of all the resources, and uses this to determine the correct order in which to create, update, or destroy resources. In this case, it will ensure the resource group is created before the virtual network.

We might wonder what happens when you delete a resource that other resources depend on. Let us say you removed the azurerm_resource_group block and then ran terraform apply. Terraform would plan to destroy both the resource group and the virtual network because the virtual network depends on the resource group.

# Summary

In this chapter, we went deeper into the practical applications that Terraform has to offer. First, we were familiar with the steps involved in installing and configuring Terraform on a Linux machine, as well as the steps necessary to ready Microsoft Azure for Terraform setups. The method of setting up Terraform entails downloading the necessary Terraform package for the system, extracting the package, and adding the Terraform binary to the PATH environment variable of the system. During the configuration of Azure, you will need to generate a service principal for Terraform. This service principal will grant Terraform the permissions necessary to handle the resources in your Azure subscription.

After that, we went over some of the fundamental commands and capabilities offered by the Terraform CLI. The Command Line Interface (CLI) serves as the primary interface for working with Terraform setups and running commands in Terraform. We were familiar with commands such as init, plan, apply, and destroy, all of which play an important part in the cycle of life for Terraform resources. In addition to this, we discussed the HashiCorp Configuration Language (HCL), which is the language used by Terraform. This language is intended to be usable by both humans and machines. It gives us the ability to build and manage resources in a declarative manner, which means that all we have to do is specify what we want, and Terraform will figure out how to get it done.

At long last, we got our hands dirty with Terraform by writing, applying, and subsequently trashing our very first Terraform configuration. In addition, we talked about the resource dependencies that are available in Terraform. These dependencies are what dictate the order in which resources are generated, modified, and removed. In our scenario, we constructed a virtual network inside of a resource group in Azure. This serves as an example of how the virtual network is dependent on the resource group. To successfully manage large infrastructures including various resources, having a good understanding of these dependencies is essential. We were able to obtain a more in-depth grasp of how Terraform operates and how it can be utilised for the management of infrastructure by participating in this hands-on event.

# CHAPTER 3: ESSENTIALS OF TERRAFORM CONFIGURATION LANGUAGE (HCL)

# HashiCorp Configuration Language In-Depth

As we begin Chapter 3, we will go deeper into the HashiCorp Configuration Language (HCL), which is essential to having a successful experience while dealing with Terraform. The primary function of HCL in Terraform is to define and supply our infrastructure resources with data in a format that is structured. The Human-Friendly Declarative Language, or HCL, is a declarative language that enables you to tell Terraform what to do without detailing the particular steps that need to be taken in order to perform the task.

HCL's major function is to specify the resources that go into the creation of our infrastructure. These resources can be higher-level components like Kubernetes clusters or lower-level components like virtual machines and network interfaces. Blocks are used to specify these resources, and within each block is a representation of a particular resource type along with any required or optional properties. In Terraform, one other essential feature of HCL is that it simplifies the process of establishing complicated connections across different infrastructure resources. For instance, the availability of a database server could be crucial to the operation of an application server. These connections may be mapped out and handled with relative ease using HCL.

In addition to managing resources, HCL offers a method of creating reusable components, often known as modules, which may be used to standardize and manage infrastructures in a more effective manner. Additionally, HCL enables the utilization of variables and outputs, which simplifies the process of tailoring Terraform setups and simplifying the exchange of information between resources or with the end user. In the end, HCL is able to bridge the gap between the non-technical (configuration) components of a project and the technical (infrastructure) aspects of the project. It gives you a high amount of control over the underlying infrastructure while allowing you to write configurations in a style that is simple to comprehend and keep up with at the same time.

Let us go on to a more in-depth discussion of the fundamentals of HCL, beginning with the language's syntax and then moving on to its primary constructs, which include resources, variables, outputs, and modules. We will also take a look at how HCL may be used to handle more advanced use cases such as loops and conditionals, both of which are essential to the process of constructing flexible and dynamic setups.

# Variables Definitions

Variables in Terraform serve as customizable elements in the Terraform configuration. They let you define values that can be reused throughout the configuration or values that can be set when the configuration is used. This is a powerful feature that enhances the reusability and modularity of Terraform configurations.

There are three types of variables you can define in Terraform: input variables, output variables, and local values. For the purpose of this discussion, we will focus on input variables.

# Defining Input Variables

Input variables serve as parameters for a Terraform module, allowing aspects of the module to be customized without altering the module's source code. They are the most common type of variable.

Following is the syntax for declaring an input variable in the Terraform configuration:

```
variable "variable_name" {
  description = "A helpful description that will be shown in the Terraform docs"
  type        = string
  default     = "default_value"
}
```

In the above syntax, variable_name is the name of the variable (you will use this to reference the variable elsewhere in the configuration), description is an optional field that can provide a description of the variable, type indicates the type of value the variable should hold (like string, list, map, bool, number or any complex type composed by these), and default is an optional field that provides a default value if none is supplied when calling the module.

# Using Input Variables

Once you've defined an input variable, you can use it elsewhere in the configuration by using the var prefix. Below is an example of how to use a variable in an azurerm_resource_group resource:

```
resource "azurerm_resource_group" "my_rg" {
  name     = var.resource_group_name
  location = var.location
}
```

In this case, var.resource_group_name and var.location are references to input variables. When Terraform interprets this configuration, it will substitute these with the actual values of the variables.

## Assigning Values to Variables

We can assign values to variables in several ways, including from a file, from the command line, from environment variables, or from Terraform Cloud/Enterprise variables.

For instance, to assign variables from a file, you'd create a terraform.tfvars file (or any file ending in .auto.tfvars) in the same directory as the configuration. This file might look something like this:

```
resource_group_name = "myResourceGroup"
location            = "West Europe"
```

When you run terraform apply, Terraform will automatically load and use variables defined in these files.

Understanding and using variables effectively is key to creating flexible, reusable Terraform configurations. By parameterizing the resources with variables, you can customize the infrastructure in countless ways without having to modify the underlying configuration.

# Interpolation Syntax

In the world of Terraform, the term interpolation refers to the process of embedding expressions within strings to produce a resultant value. In HCL, interpolation syntax is used to combine static values and variables, perform operations, call built-in functions, and reference attributes of resources and modules.

Interpolation syntax in Terraform is represented as ${...}. For example, if you have an input variable called instance_type and you want to use its value within a string, you would use the interpolation syntax as follows:

```
resource "aws_instance" "example" {
  instance_type = "${var.instance_type}"
}
```

In this case, ${var.instance_type} will be replaced with the value of the instance_type variable when the configuration is executed.

However, it's important to note that as of Terraform 0.12 and later, the interpolation syntax is optional when the placeholder stands alone. The following code will work the same way as the above example:

```
resource "aws_instance" "example" {
  instance_type = var.instance_type
}
```

This is part of a broader shift in Terraform 0.12 to improve the HCL language, and it simplifies the syntax for many common cases. However, the ${...} syntax is still required for more complex expressions or function calls.

We can also use interpolation for more complex expressions, like mathematical operations, string manipulation, or conditional logic. For instance, suppose you want to create a certain number of instances based on a condition. We could use the conditional interpolation function like so:

```
resource "aws_instance" "example" {
  count = "${var.create_instances ? var.instance_count : 0}"
}
```

In the above syntax, if var.create_instances is true, then var.instance_count instances will be created. If it's false, no instances will be created.

Furthermore, the interpolation syntax can be used to reference the attributes of resources. For example, suppose you create an AWS instance and want to capture its ID for use elsewhere. We could reference it like this:

```
output "instance_id" {
  value = "${aws_instance.example.id}"
}
```

For the purpose of this illustration, the ID of the newly formed instance will be located at aws_instance.example.id. The interpolation syntax in Terraform is a strong tool that enables users to design dynamic configurations with a high degree of flexibility.

Interpolation gives the flexibility you need to adjust the configurations to the specific use case, whether you're merging static and variable values, carrying out operations, or referencing resource properties. This is the case regardless of whether you're doing any of these things.

# Conditional Expressions

The dynamic configuration of values according to particular criteria is made possible through the use of conditional expressions. This adds a degree of dynamism and flexibility, both of which can be extremely useful for managing large infrastructures with a wide variety of requirements.

When constructing a conditional statement, the syntax condition is used - true_val: false_val. If the condition is met, then the expression will return true_val; if the condition is not met, then the expression will return false_val. This functionality is present in a wide variety of programming languages.

Let us consider a practical example where we have an input variable named create_instances that defines whether we should create AWS instances or not. Below is the sample code how you could use a conditional expression with it:

```
variable "create_instances" {
  description = "Determine whether to create instances"
  type        = bool
  default     = false
}

resource "aws_instance" "example" {
  count = var.create_instances ? 1 : 0

  // Other configuration options...
}
```

In the above sample program, the count attribute of the aws_instance resource uses a conditional expression. If var.create_instances is true, count will be 1 and an instance will be created; if it's false, count will be 0 and no instances will be created.

Conditional expressions can also be used with more complex types like lists or maps. Let us consider an example where we have an input variable named environment that determines whether we're working in a production or development environment:

```
variable "environment" {
  description = "Deployment environment"
  type       = string
  default    = "development"
}

variable "instance_type" {
  type = map
  default = {
    production  = "t2.large"
    development = "t2.micro"
  }
}

resource "aws_instance" "example" {
  instance_type = var.instance_type[var.environment]

  // Other configuration options...
}
```

In the above sample program, the instance_type attribute of the aws_instance resource uses a map combined with a conditional expression. Depending on the value of var.environment, a different instance type will be selected.

Conditional expressions become particularly powerful when combined with other language features. For instance, you can use conditional expressions inside count or for_each meta-arguments to conditionally create multiple resource instances. While it is essential to keep Terraform configurations as simple as possible, conditional expressions offer a powerful way to handle variations in infrastructure requirements, making the configurations more flexible and adaptable.

# Loops and Dynamic Blocks

Loops and dynamic blocks in Terraform provide powerful capabilities to handle repetitive and dynamic configurations in a modular way. By using for_each and dynamic blocks, we can build reusable abstractions and generate resource configurations programmatically based on variables. These constructs greatly improve the modularity, dryness, and readability of Terraform code, making it more maintainable and understandable as infrastructure grows in complexity.

## Loops

Terraform provides two primary methods for handling loops - count and for_each.

The count parameter allows you to create multiple instances of a resource. For example, if you want to create multiple AWS instances, you could do so as follows:

```
variable "instance_count" {
  description = "Number of instances to create"
  type      = number
  default   = 2
}


resource "aws_instance" "example" {
  count = var.instance_count

  // Other configuration options...
}
```

In the above sample program, the count parameter is set to var.instance_count. This means that Terraform will create var.instance_count number of AWS instances.

The for_each meta-argument allows for more complex looping scenarios, like when you need to create resources from a map or a set of strings. It assigns each element of the given map or set to a local value that can be referenced within the resource block:

```
variable "instances" {
  description = "Map of instance names and their types"
```

```
  type      = map(string)
  default   = {
    "first"  = "t2.micro"
    "second" = "t2.medium"
  }
}


resource "aws_instance" "example" {
  for_each      = var.instances
  instance_type = each.value

  // Other configuration options...
}
```

Terraform will create an AWS instance for each key-value pair in var.instances, with instance_type set to the corresponding value from the map.

## Dynamic Blocks

Dynamic blocks in Terraform allow for the creation of multiple blocks of a certain type within a resource based on a complex type (like a list or map). This can be incredibly useful for creating multiple, similar configurations within a resource.

Let us consider an example where we want to create multiple security group rules within a security group:

```
variable "ingress_rules" {
  description = "List of ingress rules"
  type        = list(object({
    from_port   = number
    to_port     = number
    protocol    = string
    cidr_blocks = list(string)
  }))
  default = [
```

```
    {
      from_port  = 80
      to_port    = 80
      protocol   = "tcp"
      cidr_blocks = ["0.0.0.0/0"]
    },
    {
      from_port  = 22
      to_port    = 22
      protocol   = "tcp"
      cidr_blocks = ["0.0.0.0/0"]
    }
  ]
}

resource "aws_security_group" "example" {
  // Other configuration options...

  dynamic "ingress" {
    for_each = var.ingress_rules
    content {
      from_port  = ingress.value.from_port
      to_port    = ingress.value.to_port
      protocol   = ingress.value.protocol
      cidr_blocks = ingress.value.cidr_blocks
    }
  }
}
```

Within the aws_security_group resource, a new ingress block is generated for each entry in the var.ingress_rules list. This demonstrates how the resource can be used. Any Terraform practitioner worth their salt should have a solid working knowledge of loops and dynamic blocks, since these features give a means of dealing with complicated, repeated, and dynamic settings in a way that is clean and easily understandable.

# Summary

Throughout the entirety of this chapter, we dove deep into the inner workings of the configuration language that Terraform uses, which is called HashiCorp Configuration Language (HCL). Our primary focus was on the power and flexibility that HCL provides to infrastructure as code practices. HCL is a fantastic choice for the high-level description of infrastructure since it is both human-readable and favorable to machines. This makes it an excellent choice. We were aware that the variables are an essential part of HCL, as they give users the ability to tailor their settings to their own needs, and we knew how to make the most of these variables.

As we proceeded in our exploration of HCL, we were familiar with conditional expressions, which enable the configuration of values depending on conditions. We also discovered that these expressions are very powerful when combined with Terraform's loop constructions, specifically count and for_each, and that this was one of the reasons for their popularity. We showed how simple it is to generate numerous copies of a resource by using the count function. The for_each function expands on this idea by providing a more nuanced way to loop over a map or a collection of strings while simultaneously generating the appropriate amount of resources.

Finally, we looked into Terraform's dynamic blocks, which add to the expressiveness of HCL's nature while also making it more dynamic. This construct makes it possible to specify several similar blocks within a resource based on complex types such as lists or maps, which is a skill that is particularly valuable when working with larger and more sophisticated configurations. All of these components of HCL come together to make a formidable mix that enables the building of very dynamic Terraform setups that are also reusable and modular.

# CHAPTER 4:
# TERRAFORM MODULES AND REUSABLE INFRASTRUCTURE

# Introduction to Reusable Infrastructure

The introduction of cloud computing has had a profound effect on the way in which businesses conceive of, construct, and maintain their information technology infrastructure. In an era in which the speedy delivery of applications and the agility of businesses are both essential for maintaining a competitive advantage, businesses are always looking for new methods to improve the efficiency, scalability, and repeatability of their infrastructure processes. This requirement is especially pressing for larger businesses, which frequently have to maintain complicated infrastructures that are dispersed over a number of different settings, countries, or even cloud providers. The idea of reusing existing infrastructure then comes into play.

In its most basic form, the concept of reusable infrastructure refers to the capacity to construct infrastructure parts in such a way that they are capable of being used repeatedly across a variety of contexts, applications, or projects without the need to continuously redefine or reengineer those elements. This strategy enables organizations to build standardized, predetermined sets of resources that are capable of being supplied and deprovisioned according to the requirements of the project, hence reducing the amount of time and effort required.

The ideas of Infrastructure as Code (IaC) form the basis for the construction of reusable infrastructure. IaC makes it possible to create and manage infrastructure using code, which can then be version controlled, tested, and reused in a manner very similar to that of software code. The goal is to manage infrastructure in a manner similar to that of developing software by treating it as though it were software and applying the same practices and methodology. The adoption of reusable infrastructure confers a plethora of positive benefits. To start, it makes a big difference in terms of efficiency. The time it takes to bring a product to market can be cut down significantly by using pre-defined code templates to rapidly deploy environments rather than having teams manually configure each environment. Scalability is another aspect that benefits from this efficiency. When an organization expands, the underlying infrastructure needs to be able to accommodate the expansion. When you have infrastructure that is designed to be reused, scaling becomes as simple as deploying new instances of the components that constitute the infrastructure.

Second, it helps to maintain consistency while also cutting down on errors. Organizations are able to ensure that each environment is configured consistently if they use the same infrastructure definitions across environments. This reduces the likelihood of inconsistencies and configuration drift occurring inside the organization. Maintaining this consistency is absolutely necessary in order to guarantee that environments used for testing and staging appropriately represent production environments.

Thirdly, having an infrastructure that can be reused is helpful for cost control. Organizations can prevent over-provisioning of resources and improve their ability to accurately track their infrastructure usage and expenses if they define and deploy only the resources that are actually needed.

Last but not least, infrastructure that can be reused encourages team collaboration and speeds up the learning process. When infrastructure is specified as code, it possesses many of the same characteristics of software code, including the ability to be shared, evaluated, and worked upon by several teams. Teams are able to increase their capabilities, learn from one another, and create innovation when they take a collaborative approach to problem solving. In a digital ecosystem that is always shifting and developing at a quick pace, the use of reusable infrastructure is no longer a luxury but rather a must. It is a crucial enabler for businesses who want to innovate quickly, improve their operational efficiency, and become more agile in their company operations.

# Terraform Modules

Modules serve as the primary mechanism for enclosing and reusing infrastructure-related code within the framework of Terraform, which is a cloud-computing platform. They are independent bundles of Terraform configurations that group together a set of resources and act as models for the construction of reusable components of infrastructure.

A module in Terraform is a container for multiple resources that are used together. These resources could include virtual machines, security groups, network interfaces, or even complete multi-tier application stacks spread across multiple cloud providers. By packaging these resources into a module, you can define them once and reuse them multiple times in different contexts without having to duplicate the code.

Every Terraform configuration you write actually makes use of a root module, even if you haven't explicitly defined one. The root module consists of the resources defined in the .tf files in the main working directory. However, the real power of modules lies in their ability to be called by other modules, effectively allowing you to create a hierarchical structure for the infrastructure. This allows for a high degree of flexibility and scalability in defining and managing the infrastructure.

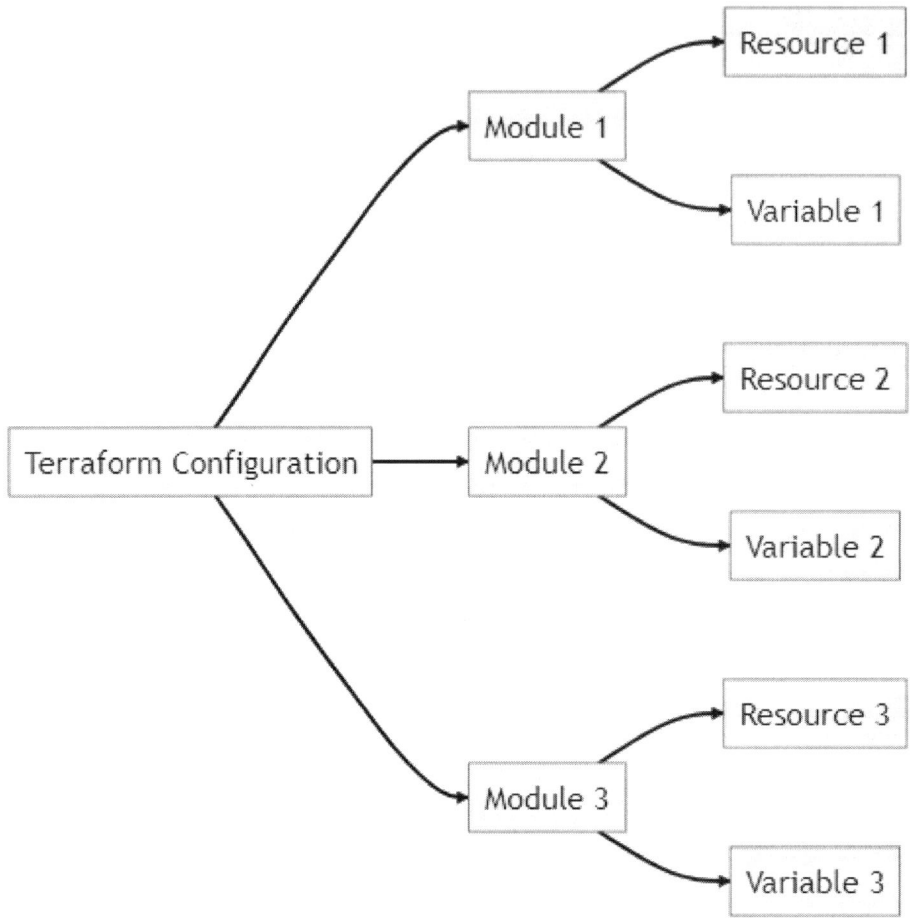

**Fig 4.1 Concept of Terraform Modules**

To illustrate, let us consider an example. Suppose you're tasked with managing the infrastructure for a web application which includes an EC2 instance and a security group in AWS. We can define a module for this stack of resources:

```
module "web" {
  source  = "./modules/web"
  version = "1.0.0"

  instance_type = "t2.micro"
  ami_id        = "ami-abc123"
```

```
  // other parameters...
}
```

In this case, the source argument tells Terraform where to find the module's resources, which are defined in the ./modules/web directory relative to the working directory. The version argument specifies the version of the module to use, and the rest of the arguments (instance_type, ami_id, etc.) are variables that the module expects.

Under the hood, when Terraform initializes the configuration, it downloads and installs any modules the configuration uses. It then incorporates these modules into its resource graph, which it uses to determine the order in which to create, update, or destroy resources. We can also use modules to organize the Terraform code and make it easier to understand, manage, and version. Modules can be shared across teams within an organization, or even publicly, leading to collaboration and reuse of infrastructure patterns. They can be version controlled separately from the main configuration, allowing you to test and promote changes to modules independently.

# Module Inputs

Module inputs, or variables, are a fundamental aspect of Terraform modules, allowing you to customize the behavior of a module each time it's used. These inputs enable the module to accept arguments, much like a function in a programming language, and make the module adaptable to various usage scenarios.

Inputs define what data is accepted by the module. They are declared within the module using the variable keyword, followed by the variable name and a block defining properties such as description, type, and default value. For instance, in our web module example from the previous discussion, we may have these input variables:

```
variable "instance_type" {
  description = "The type of instance to start."
  type     = string
  default   = "t2.micro"
}

variable "ami_id" {
  description = "The ID of the Amazon Machine Image (AMI) to use."
```

```
  type     = string
}
```

In the above syntax, the instance_type and ami_id variables allow users to customize the EC2 instance's properties. The description property provides an explanation of the variable's purpose, the type specifies what kind of data the variable accepts (in this case, string), and default specifies a default value that will be used if none is provided when calling the module.

When using the module, you can pass values to these inputs as arguments:

```
module "web" {
  source  = "./modules/web"
  version = "1.0.0"

  instance_type = "t2.small"
  ami_id       = "ami-def456"
}
```

In the above snippet, we're overriding the default instance_type and providing an ami_id for the module to use. Terraform will use these values to customize the creation of the resources defined within the module. Module inputs offer a way to abstract the complexity of a module's implementation by providing a clear, consistent API. By encapsulating details and exposing only what's necessary for customization, inputs make modules easier to use and understand.

One of the main advantages of using module inputs is their ability to enhance the reusability and flexibility of Terraform configurations. With inputs, you can use the same module to create resources with different properties. For example, you can use the web module to create instances of different sizes, in different regions, or with different AMIs, simply by changing the values passed to the module inputs. Inputs also improve the readability and maintainability of Terraform code by reducing repetition and making it explicit what data a module uses. Moreover, by utilizing rich types and validation rules, you can ensure that the module inputs are used correctly, thereby reducing potential errors and inconsistencies.

# Module Locals

Locals in Terraform are a way to define a reusable expression that may be used numerous times within a module without having to duplicate the expression. This is accomplished by avoiding the need to copy and paste the expression. The usage of locals can be particularly helpful for reducing the complexity of expressions and making the Terraform setup easier to comprehend and maintain.

A local value can be defined inside of a module by using the locals block, which is then followed by one or more local names and the expressions that correspond to those names. The syntax looks like this:

```
locals {
  local_name = expression
}
```

The expression can be any valid Terraform expression, and the resulting value can be used throughout the module using the syntax local.local_name.

Consider an example where we're managing a set of web servers in AWS, and we want to construct a standard naming convention for our instances:

```
locals {
  instance_name = "web-${var.environment}-${var.region}"
}
```

In the above syntax, the local instance_name constructs a name using the environment and region variables. We can then use local.instance_name anywhere in our module where we need to refer to this name.

One advantage of using locals is that it makes the code more DRY (Don't Repeat Yourself). If we need to change the naming convention, we only have to change it in one place, not every place the name is used. Locals can also simplify complex expressions. Consider a case where you need to compute a value based on the result of a conditional expression:

```
locals {
  subnet_id = var.environment == "prod" ? var.prod_subnet_id :
var.dev_subnet_id
```

```
}
```

This local subnet_id will hold the ID of the production subnet if the environment variable is "prod", otherwise it will hold the ID of the development subnet. We can use local.subnet_id wherever we need to refer to the subnet ID, making our resource configurations cleaner and easier to read.

Furthermore, locals are great for handling optional module input variables. If you have an input variable that is optional and doesn't have a default value, you can use a local to provide a fallback value. Below is an example:

```
variable "instance_type" {
  description = "The type of instance to start."
  type       = string
}

locals {
  instance_type = var.instance_type != null ? var.instance_type : "t2.micro"
}
```

In this scenario, "t2.micro" will be used as the default value for local.instance_type if var.instance_type is not supplied when the module is invoked. To summarize, locals are a helpful utility available via the Terraform programming language. They make it possible for you to simplify complex expressions, generate expressions that can be reused, and increase the code's readability and maintainability in Terraform. We will be able to generate Terraform configurations that are cleaner, more efficient, and easier to comprehend if you make appropriate use of locals.

# Module Outputs

Module outputs in Terraform act as a way to expose certain values that result from the module's execution. Just like a function in a programming language, after processing its logic, it returns a value or multiple values. In the Terraform world, those are referred to as outputs. Outputs are an essential part of Terraform modules, and they allow us to capture and pass along information between modules and from modules back up to the root module.

Module outputs are defined with the output keyword followed by an identifier, and they usually contain a value attribute that determines what data will be output from the module. Following is an example:

```
output "instance_id" {
  description = "The ID of the created instance."
  value      = aws_instance.web.id
}
```

In the above syntax, the output keyword defines an output named instance_id. The value of this output is the ID of the EC2 instance created within this module (aws_instance.web.id).

The description attribute is optional and provides an explanation of the output's purpose. This can be especially useful when working with complex modules or collaborating with other developers. Once defined, outputs can be accessed from outside the module using the syntax module.<MODULE_NAME>.<OUTPUT_NAME>. Below is a sample demonstration:

```
module "web" {
  source  = "./modules/web"
  version = "1.0.0"
}

output "web_instance_id" {
  value = module.web.instance_id
}
```

In this case, we're using a module named "web", and then outputting the instance_id of the created instance for use elsewhere in our configuration or for display when terraform apply is run. Outputs are also how information gets transmitted back to the user when Terraform runs. When you run terraform apply, Terraform will display the value of any output blocks in the root module, giving you a handy way to display important information like resource identifiers, login credentials, or IP addresses. A powerful use case for outputs is to expose a subset of a resource's attributes, as a way of defining a controlled API for the module. This allows you to hide the complexity of a resource and expose only the necessary attributes.

For example, you might have a module that creates an AWS RDS instance, which has many attributes, but perhaps you only want to expose the endpoint and port:

```
resource "aws_db_instance" "default" {
  allocated_storage    = 10
  engine               = "mysql"
  engine_version       = "5.7"
  instance_class       = "db.t2.micro"
  name                 = "mydb"
  username             = "foo"
  password             = "foobarbaz"
  parameter_group_name = "default.mysql5.7"
}

output "endpoint" {
  description = "The connection endpoint."
  value       = aws_db_instance.default.endpoint
}

output "port" {
  description = "The database port."
  value       = aws_db_instance.default.port
}
```

Controlling the information that is made available to module users is one of the primary functions of outputs; this enables outputs to contribute to making modules reusable and manageable. In closing, outputs are a key tool in Terraform that allows users to convey results, make ties between modules, and structure the output of resources and modules in a way that is clean and structured. Moreover, outputs also allow users to establish links between Terraform and other systems.

# Write My First Module

Let us start creating our first module. For this, we will use a practical example and create a module that will manage an Azure Virtual Network (VNet). The Azure Virtual Network service enables Azure resources to communicate with each other securely.

To get started, let us define the directory structure. Terraform will load all .tf files in the module's directory, so it's common to split the configuration into multiple files. Following is how you might lay out the files for this module:

```
modules/
    └── azure_vnet/
        ├── main.tf
        ├── variables.tf
        ├── outputs.tf
```

main.tf will contain the main set of configuration for the module. variables.tf will define any input variables the module requires, and outputs.tf will define any values the module outputs. Let us start with variables.tf. In the below sample program, we will define the input variables that our module will accept:

```
variable "resource_group_name" {
  description = "Name of the resource group"
  type     = string
}

variable "location" {
  description = "Azure region location"
  type     = string
}

variable "vnet_name" {
  description = "Name of the virtual network"
  type     = string
}

variable "address_space" {
  description = "Address space of the virtual network"
  type     = list(string)
```

```
}
```

These variables will allow us to pass in the necessary information to create the virtual network in the correct location and with the correct properties. Now, let us move to main.tf, which will contain the main logic of our module:

```
resource "azurerm_virtual_network" "vnet" {
  name                = var.vnet_name
  resource_group_name = var.resource_group_name
  location            = var.location
  address_space       = var.address_space
}
```

This code creates an Azure Virtual Network using the azurerm_virtual_network resource type. The required attributes are populated from our input variables. Finally, we want to define some outputs for our module in the outputs.tf file:

```
output "vnet_id" {
  description = "The ID of the created virtual network."
  value       = azurerm_virtual_network.vnet.id
}

output "vnet_address_space" {
  description = "The address space of the created virtual network."
  value       = azurerm_virtual_network.vnet.address_space
}
```

These output values will allow us to capture and use the ID and address space of the created virtual network elsewhere in our Terraform configuration. Now that we've defined our module, we can call it from our main configuration file:

```
module "vnet" {
```

```
source                = "./modules/azure_vnet"
resource_group_name   = "my-resource-group"
location              = "West Europe"
vnet_name             = "my-vnet"
address_space         = ["10.0.0.0/16"]
}
```

In this instance, we are making a call to our azure_vnet module by utilizing the module block. After passing the necessary variables into the module, our module will now build a virtual network in the location, resource group, and name and address space that have been supplied by the user. And that wraps things up! We have completed the writing of our first module. We have made the logic to build a virtual network reusable across a number of different environments or projects by encapsulating it within this module, and we have also ensured that the parameters remain consistent. We can make our Terraform code more organized, which will make it easier to read and maintain, and we can break up our infrastructure into modules to accomplish these goals.

# Nested Modules

Terraform nested modules allow us to further encapsulate infrastructure by defining modules within modules. It lets us break down a complex system into smaller, more manageable chunks, and promotes code reuse.

Consider a scenario where we need to create an Azure Virtual Network (VNet) and also a subnet within that VNet. We have already created a module for Azure VNet in the previous example. Now, let us build a new module for creating a subnet and then nest this subnet module within our VNet module.

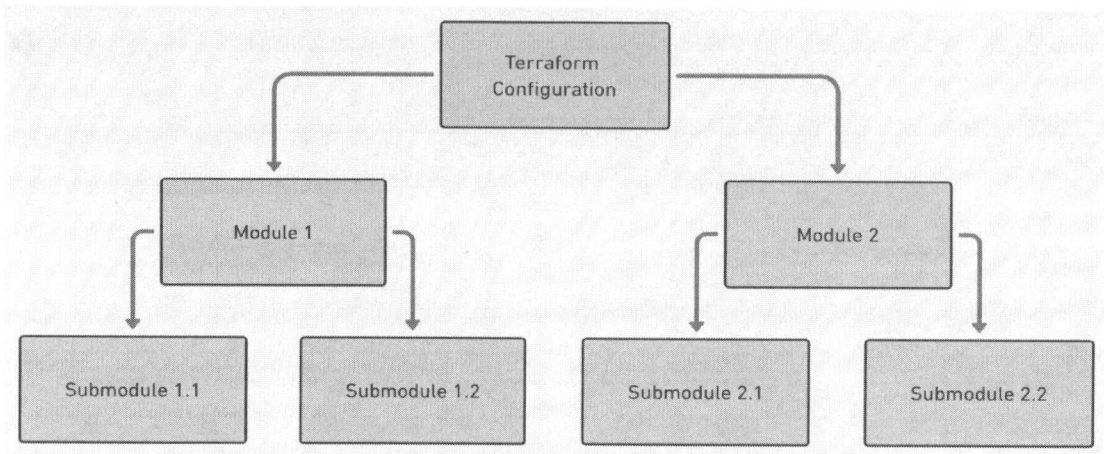

**Fig 4.2 Nested Modules**

To start, create a new directory under the modules directory named azure_subnet. Then, create main.tf, variables.tf, and outputs.tf files in this directory:

```
modules/
    ├── azure_vnet/
    │    ├── main.tf
    │    ├── variables.tf
    │    ├── outputs.tf
    └── azure_subnet/
         ├── main.tf
         ├── variables.tf
         ├── outputs.tf
```

In variables.tf, define the input variables required for creating a subnet:

```
variable "resource_group_name" {
  description = "Name of the resource group"
  type      = string
}

variable "vnet_name" {
  description = "Name of the virtual network"
```

66

```
  type      = string
}

variable "subnet_name" {
  description = "Name of the subnet"
  type      = string
}

variable "subnet_address_prefix" {
  description = "Address prefix of the subnet"
  type      = string
}
```

In main.tf, write the code to create a subnet using the azurerm_subnet resource type:

```
resource "azurerm_subnet" "subnet" {
  name               = var.subnet_name
  resource_group_name  = var.resource_group_name
  virtual_network_name = var.vnet_name
  address_prefix      = var.subnet_address_prefix
}
```

In outputs.tf, define the ID of the created subnet as an output:

```
  description = "The ID of the created subnet"
  value     = azurerm_subnet.subnet.id
}
```

We now have a module for creating a subnet. To nest this module within the VNet module, open the main.tf file under azure_vnet and add a module block to call the azure_subnet module:

```
module "subnet" {
  source            = "../azure_subnet"
```

```
resource_group_name  = var.resource_group_name
vnet_name            = var.vnet_name
subnet_name          = "my-subnet"
subnet_address_prefix = "10.0.1.0/24"
}
```

This block utilizes the azure_subnet module to create a subnet within the virtual network defined by the azure_vnet module. The relative path ../azure_subnet specifies the location of the azure_subnet module source.

By nesting modules in this way, we can provision an entire network architecture composed of a VNet and subnet just by calling the parent azure_vnet module. The child azure_subnet module is referenced from there. This modular composition promotes code reusability and organization. Network components can be defined once in their own modules, then composed together in different configurations. Overall, nesting modules results in Terraform code that is more modular and maintainable. Complex infrastructure can be built up from nested modules each encapsulating a single element.

# Implement Module Versioning

In Terraform, the versioning of modules enables you to manage changes in a structured and predictable manner. This is particularly useful when a module is being used across different environments or projects, and you need to introduce new features or make changes without impacting existing deployments.

For versioning to work, you must host the Terraform module on a supported platform like GitHub, Bitbucket, or the Terraform Registry. These platforms provide version control systems that are essential for versioning to work. Let us assume we are using GitHub.

Following is an overview of the steps involved:

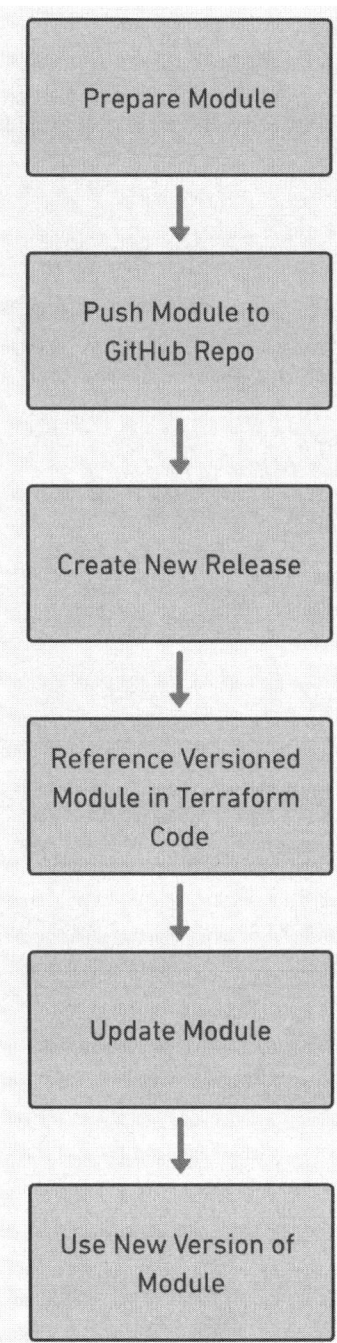

**Fig 4.3 Steps to Implement Model Versioning**

# Preparing Module Locally

First, we'll want to develop the module code locally before publishing it. Each module should be self-contained within its own dedicated directory. This allows it to be transported easily.

The module directory should include all the Terraform configuration files necessary to provision the resources related to that module. For example, an Azure virtual network module would contain .tf files for the resource group, vnet, subnets, etc. Be sure to parameterize inputs and expose outputs so the module can be customized and interfaced with other components. Encapsulate the module functionality fully before publishing.

# Pushing Module to GitHub

Once the module code is complete, we need to host it in a version control system that is accessible to our Terraform codebase. GitHub is a great choice for publishing reusable modules. Create a new GitHub repository to contain the module code. The repository can be named similarly to the module, like terraform-azure-vnet for an Azure virtual network module.

With the repository created, push the local module directory to GitHub. Now the module code is hosted in a centralized, shared location.

# Creating Releases to Version the Module

One of the key benefits of leveraging GitHub is the ability to version modules using releases. GitHub releases provide Git tags and changelog tracking for module versions.

To create a new release, navigate to the "Releases" section of the GitHub repository. Click the "Draft a new release" button. Give the release a semantic version tag like v1.0.0. Semantic versioning provides a standardized naming convention for module versions.

In the release notes, describe the contents of this version - new features, fixes, changes etc. This informs consumers. When ready, click "Publish release" to make the versioned module available for use.

# Consuming the Versioned Module

With the module hosted and versioned on GitHub, we can now easily reference it from our Terraform configurations. In the Terraform code, use a module block to specify the source and version:

```
module "vnet" {
 source = "github.com/username/terraform-azure-vnet?ref=v1.0.0"
 # parameters..
}
```

The source parameter points to the GitHub repository containing the module. The ref parameter pins the version to use - in this case v1.0.0.

Now when we run Terraform commands, it will fetch version v1.0.0 of the module from the GitHub source. Module versions allow reproducible Terraform runs.

## Updating the Module

When we need to make enhancements or fixes to the module, we work in the GitHub repository to update the module code. Commit the changes and create a new release incrementing the version number according to semantic versioning rules - for example v1.1.0 for new functionality.

The new version can be consumed by updating the ref parameter in Terraform configurations to point to the latest release. Existing users will continue running previous versions until ready to upgrade.

This module development and versioning approach provides many benefits:

- Reusability - Modules encapsulate and package infrastructure for easy reuse
- Portability - Modules can be easily distributed and consumed
- Maintainability - Modules have a centralized source of truth in version control
- Collaboration - Teams can build and publish shared modules
- Stability - Module versions prevent breaking upstream dependencies

Overall, developing reusable, versioned modules is a best practice that improves many aspects of infrastructure management with Terraform. By open sourcing modules on GitHub, we can maximize sharing, collaboration and reusability across our organization.

# Summary

In the fourth chapter, we dove deep into the idea of reusable infrastructure and investigated the reasons why it is such an important component of modern DevOps practices. Terraform improves the capacity of developers to handle complicated infrastructures by enclosing infrastructure logic within modules that can be reused and for which versions can be controlled. The advantages of taking such an approach are various, and they include a reduction in the amount of code that is duplicated, an increase in maintainability, an ease in testing and debugging, and an improvement in team collaboration. The concept of infrastructure as code is advanced when reusable modules are used since this creates a language that can be communicated between different teams.

The idea of Terraform modules was one of the most important topics covered in this chapter. We investigated the manner in which modules, at their fundamental level, enclose a collection of infrastructure resources that can be used together. Within Terraform, they serve as a core unit of organization, assisting in the simplification of setups and encouraging reuse. We gained an understanding of the operation of modules by focusing on its three fundamental components: inputs, locals, and outputs. While Locals offer a means to simplify complicated expressions that are contained within the module, Inputs give the user the ability to modify the behavior of the module. The technique for exposing specific values outside of the module to other configurations or the user is called an output. These data can then be used by other configurations or queried by the user.

After that, we put this information to use in the real world by developing a fundamental module for an Azure environment. We examined the practical application of nested modules as a means of further modularizing infrastructure components after gaining an understanding of how to define, reference, and apply modules. The configuration will be much simpler to comprehend and administer if you use nested modules since they produce a hierarchical structure that is analogous to the structure of the system you are developing.

In the final part of this discussion, we dug into the idea of module versioning. This method makes it easier to manage changes to the infrastructure without disrupting the environment in which operations are taking place. We learned how to implement version control by observing how modules are managed when they are hosted on services like GitHub. We were familiar with the processes of preparing a module for versioning, submitting it to a repository on GitHub, producing a new release, and referencing the versioned module in Terraform code. We also investigated how to upgrade a module and switch to a new version without causing any disruption to the deployments that are already in place. In conclusion, the information presented in this chapter provided a comprehensive comprehension of reusable infrastructure and Terraform modules, as well as their administration and practical applications.

# CHAPTER 5: TERRAFORM STATE MANAGEMENT

# Understanding Terraform State

The Terraform state is an essential part of Terraform's design. It's a JSON file that Terraform generates automatically when managing resources. The state file (usually named terraform.tfstate) contains information about the resources that Terraform has created or managed, as well as configuration details and dependency data.

One of the primary reasons the state file exists is to map real-world resources to the configuration. When you create a resource using Terraform, it records all the relevant information about that resource in the state file. Then, during future runs, Terraform compares the current state of the actual resource with the desired state defined in the configuration and makes the necessary changes to match the desired state.

Another key function of the state file is to store metadata about the resources, such as resource dependencies. This is important for determining the order in which changes need to be applied, which can be crucial when dealing with complex infrastructure setups with many interdependent resources. One way to think about the state is as a snapshot of the managed infrastructure at a point in time. Just as a version control system uses a diff between file versions to determine changes, Terraform uses the difference between the configuration and the state file to decide what changes are required.

For example, if you have an Azure virtual network defined in the Terraform configuration, the state file will hold details like its ID, name, address space, and any other attribute that Terraform can ascertain about that resource. Suppose you change the address space in the Terraform configuration and run a terraform apply. In that case, Terraform will compare the desired configuration with the state file, notice the difference, and carry out the necessary API calls to Azure to align the actual state of the resource with the desired state.

However, the state file also presents a couple of challenges. Firstly, it can contain sensitive information as it holds a complete snapshot of the infrastructure. Hence, it's crucial to handle it securely. Secondly, when working in a team environment, maintaining a consistent state file can be tricky. The state file should be in sync for all team members, ensuring everyone has a consistent view of the infrastructure. For this, we use remote state, which allows the state file to be stored on a shared storage backend like Azure Blob Storage, AWS S3, or HashiCorp's own Terraform Cloud.

# Local vs Remote State

When managing infrastructure with Terraform, understanding the concepts of local and remote state is critical. As we've discussed, the state file is a fundamental part of how Terraform operates. It allows Terraform to map the real-world resources to the configuration, keep track of metadata, and manage dependencies. The choice between using a local state or a remote state depends primarily on the working environment and the level of collaboration within the team.

# Local State

In its simplest form, Terraform stores its state file on the local disk. This is known as local state. Whenever you run Terraform commands like terraform apply or terraform plan, Terraform reads the current state from this local file and updates it after applying changes. For individual developers working on personal projects, or in situations where there's no need for collaboration, the local state can be a straightforward and efficient approach.

However, using local state has its limitations, particularly when we start working in a team-oriented, collaborative environment. Multiple people working on the same infrastructure can quickly lead to state conflicts if everyone is maintaining a separate local state file. Also, since the state file might contain sensitive information, having it reside on individual's local systems could pose a security risk.

# Remote State

The solution to these challenges comes in the form of a remote state. With remote state, the state file is stored in a shared, central location, such as Azure Blob Storage, AWS S3, Google Cloud Storage, or HashiCorp's own Terraform Cloud. This approach offers several significant benefits over local states.

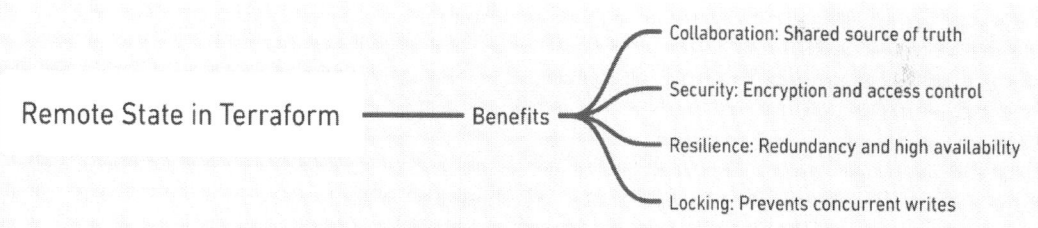

**Fig 5.1 Remote State in Terraform**

## *Collaboration*
Having a single, shared source of truth for the infrastructure state is crucial in a team environment. It ensures everyone is working with the latest state and reduces the risk of conflicts and inconsistencies.

## *Security*
Storing the state file remotely allows you to take advantage of the security features offered

by the remote storage providers, like encryption at rest and in transit. We can also control who has access to the state file and maintain an audit trail of who made which changes.

## Resilience

Remote storage solutions often provide redundancy and high availability, reducing the risk of losing the state file due to disk failures or other local issues.

## Locking

Many remote backends support state locking, a feature that prevents multiple concurrent writes to the state file. This feature is essential to prevent corruption or conflicts in the state file during concurrent runs.

To use a remote state, you define a backend in the Terraform configuration. This backend block specifies the remote storage service you want to use and the necessary details to connect to it. Once set up, running Terraform commands as you usually would now interact with the remote state. In summary, while the local state may be sufficient for single-user, non-critical infrastructures, it has several drawbacks when it comes to collaboration, security, and resilience. On the other hand, the remote state addresses these challenges, making it more suitable for production-grade, team-based infrastructure management. Choosing the correct type of state management is a significant step in effectively using Terraform.

# Implementing Remote State in Terraform Configuration

In order to save the state file after implementing the remote state in our Terraform setup, you will need to make sure that you have an Azure storage account that is already set up and ready to go. In addition to that, we'll need a storage container to be included in this account. We can make these through the Azure site or the Azure command line interface.

Let us walk through the process of setting up Terraform to use a remote state that is saved in Azure Blob Storage. For the below illustration, we'll assume that you already have a storage account and a container.

## Define the Backend

The first step in implementing a remote state is to define a backend configuration in the Terraform files. Open the main.tf file, or whatever file you're using for the Terraform configuration, and add a terraform block with a backend sub-block. For Azure, you'd use the azurerm backend type:

```
terraform {
  backend "azurerm" {
    resource_group_name  = "terraformstate"
    storage_account_name = "terraformstate123"
    container_name       = "tfstate"
    key                  = "terraform.tfstate"
  }
}
```

This backend block tells Terraform to store its state in an Azure Storage container. We will need to replace the resource_group_name, storage_account_name, and container_name with the specific Azure storage details.

The key parameter is the name of the state file that Terraform will create in the Azure Blob Storage container.

## Initialize the Backend

With the backend defined, you'll need to reinitialize the Terraform workspace. Run terraform init:

```
$ terraform init
```

During the initialization process, Terraform will set up the Azure backend and migrate any existing state to the new backend. If you have an existing local state file, Terraform will ask if you want to copy that state to the new backend. Answering "yes" will migrate the state.

## Verify the Remote State

Now that the remote state is set up, you can verify it's working by running terraform apply. Once the operation completes, you should see the state file in the Azure Storage container. We can check this using the Azure portal or Azure CLI.

We can also pull the state file locally for inspection using terraform state pull:

```
$ terraform state pull
```

This will output the contents of the current state file to the terminal.

## Working with Remote State

From this point forward, any changes made to the infrastructure using terraform apply or terraform destroy will update the state file in the Azure Storage container.

Also, if you are working in a team, the colleagues can set up their Terraform environment with the same backend configuration. This will ensure everyone is working off the same state, reducing the risk of conflicts and inconsistencies.

To summarize, in order to use a remote state in Azure with Terraform, you will first need to define a backend in the Terraform configuration, and then you will need to reinitialize the workspace. After it has been configured, Terraform will automatically manage the state file in the remote location. This will result in the infrastructure state having a single authoritative source.

# State Manipulation

State manipulation refers to the ability to modify the Terraform state manually. This is generally necessary in situations where automated processes can't resolve specific issues or when you need to manage resources that weren't initially created by Terraform.

However, manual state manipulation should be done very carefully. Improper modifications can lead to inconsistencies between the actual infrastructure and the Terraform state, which can result in unexpected Terraform behaviors.

## Modes to Manipulate State

Following are the primary methods for managing and manipulating the state in Terraform or similar infrastructure as code tools:

### Terraform State RM

This command is used to remove items from the Terraform state. Suppose you've manually deleted a resource outside of Terraform, and now Terraform wants to recreate it, but you want Terraform to forget it. In such a case, you can use the terraform state rm command to remove the resource from the state file.

```
terraform state rm azurerm_resource_group.rg
```

This will remove the resource named "rg" of type "azurerm_resource_group" from the state.

## Terraform State MV

If you want to rename a resource or move it to a different module, you can use terraform state mv. This is useful when you're refactoring the Terraform configuration files and need to ensure the state matches the updated configuration. The general usage is:

```
terraform state mv [options] SOURCE DESTINATION
```

Below is a sample code of moving a resource to a module:

```
terraform state mv azurerm_resource_group.rg module.example
```

## Terraform State Pull/Push

In rare cases, you might need to manually edit the state file. Terraform allows you to pull the state file, modify it, and then push it back. Check out the below snippet:

```
terraform state pull > terraform.tfstate
```

This will output the state to a local file named "terraform.tfstate". We can then open this file in a text editor, make the necessary changes, and push it back using:

```
terraform state push terraform.tfstate
```

Keep in mind that manual editing should only be used as a last resort. Always make sure to backup the state file before performing any manual changes.

## Terraform Refresh

Terraform refresh is another form of state manipulation. This command is used to reconcile the state Terraform knows about (via its state file) with the real-world infrastructure. It does this by querying the provider to learn the current values of a resource. After running terraform refresh, Terraform updates the state file to reflect the actual infrastructure setup.

```
terraform refresh
```

To sum up, Terraform's state manipulation is a potent tool because it permits manual involvement in the state file. In spite of the fact that it could be useful, it is strongly advised that these commands not be used carelessly because their incorrect use could result in a corrupted state file or incompatibilities between the infrastructure and the state.

# State Conflicts

State conflicts in Terraform typically arise in situations where multiple team members are working on the same infrastructure simultaneously, or when there are manual changes to the infrastructure outside of Terraform. These situations lead to inconsistencies between the actual infrastructure and the Terraform state file, causing conflicts when Terraform attempts to apply changes.

Let us proceed to explore some common situations of conflicts and how to resolve them:

## Concurrent Terraform Operations

When multiple team members execute Terraform commands concurrently, they might encounter state lock errors. Terraform uses state locking to prevent others from running Terraform commands that could conflict. However, in some scenarios, the lock might not be released, leading to a conflict.

To resolve this, you can manually unlock the state file using the terraform force-unlock command. However, it's essential to be sure that the previous Terraform operation is indeed not running as forcing the unlock can cause state corruption.

```
terraform force-unlock LOCK_ID
```

## Drift Management

Drift happens when the actual infrastructure setup diverges from the state stored in the Terraform state file. This can occur when changes are made to the infrastructure outside of Terraform, such as manual modifications or automated processes.

To manage and correct drift, you can use the terraform refresh command to update the state file with the actual infrastructure state. After the state file is updated, terraform plan can show the difference between the current state and the desired state. If the drift is acceptable, the state file can be left as is. If not, you can use terraform apply to reconcile the differences.

## Manual Changes to State File

If you've manually edited the state file and inadvertently introduced conflicts or errors, the terraform validate command can be used to check the syntax of the Terraform files, and terraform plan can be used to check the state file's validity.

In case of an error, you can restore the state from a backup if available. If not, you might need to manually fix the state file or use the terraform state rm command to remove the problematic resources and import them back using terraform import.

## Inconsistent Resource Metadata

Sometimes, Terraform may fail to apply changes due to inconsistencies between resource metadata in the state file and the actual configuration files. This can occur when moving or renaming resources or modules without using the appropriate commands.

In such situations, you can use the terraform state mv command to correctly rename or move the resources in the state file. This command updates the state file to reflect the new location or name of the resource, resolving the conflict.

It's crucial to understand that resolving state conflicts requires careful analysis of the situation. It is always recommended to use the appropriate Terraform commands to manage state and avoid manual interventions unless absolutely necessary. Regularly backing up the state file can also be a lifesaver when dealing with state conflicts.

# State Drift and Reconciliation

In the realm of Terraform, the term "drift" is used to denote any divergence between the actual state of the infrastructure and the state recorded in the Terraform state file. The phenomenon of drift may occur due to multiple reasons such as manual changes to the infrastructure outside of Terraform, automatic updates made by cloud providers, or even inadvertent modifications due to software bugs.

## How State Drift Occurs?

Drift management is a critical part of maintaining infrastructure as code, as the undetected or unmanaged drift can lead to unpredictable Terraform behavior, unforeseen dependencies, or discrepancies in reporting. It is also essential for compliance and governance, as infrastructure drift might lead to potential vulnerabilities and security breaches.

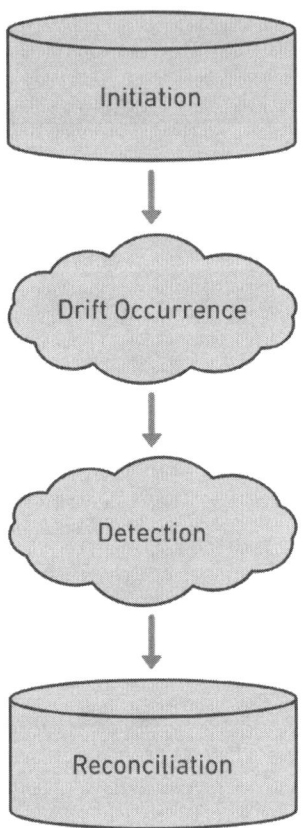

**Fig 5.2 Process of Drift Occurence in Terraform**

Following is a step-by-step overview of how drift can occur:

- Initiation: We use Terraform to create or update infrastructure. Once the terraform apply command is executed, Terraform stores the current state of the infrastructure in the state file.

- Drift Occurrence: Changes are made to the infrastructure outside of Terraform. This could be manual changes, such as someone modifying a virtual machine's settings in the Azure portal, or automated changes, such as an auto-scaling policy increasing the number of instances.

- Detection: The next time you run terraform plan or terraform apply, Terraform compares the desired state (as defined by the Terraform configuration) with the current state (as defined by the state file) and the actual state (the real infrastructure). In this process, Terraform detects the drift – any difference between the actual state and the current state.

- Reconciliation of the drift in Terraform can be achieved by using the terraform refresh command followed by terraform apply. The refresh command updates the state file with the actual state of the infrastructure, allowing you to see the drift when you run terraform plan.

```
# Update the state file with the real infrastructure
terraform refresh

# Check the differences between the desired, current and actual state
terraform plan
```

Once you've assessed the changes presented by the plan command, you can decide whether to:

1. Reconcile the Drift Automatically: If the drift is acceptable or expected (e.g., an auto-scaling event), you might just want to update the state file to match the actual infrastructure. Running terraform apply will align the state file with the desired state and actual infrastructure state.

2. Undo the Drift Manually: If the drift was due to an unauthorized or undesirable change, you might need to manually revert the change in the infrastructure and then run terraform refresh to update the state file.

In summary, state drift is a common scenario in managing infrastructure, especially in dynamic and shared environments. Using tools like Terraform for drift detection and reconciliation helps maintain infrastructure consistency, reduces troubleshooting complexity, and enhances overall operational efficiency.

# State Migration

State migration in Terraform refers to the process of moving resources within or between Terraform states. The need for state migration arises under several circumstances, including but not limited to:

1. Refactoring Terraform Configurations: As the infrastructure grows and changes, you might need to reorganize the Terraform configurations for better manageability or modularity. Such refactoring may involve moving resources from one

configuration (or module) to another, which requires state migration to avoid destroying and recreating the same resources.

2. Adopting Remote State Storage: If you initially use local state storage and later decide to switch to remote state storage for collaboration or security reasons, you need to migrate the state from the local backend to the remote backend.

3. Switching Between Remote Backends: For instance, you may want to switch from an Azure Blob Storage backend to a Terraform Cloud backend due to organization policy changes or service upgrades. This also involves state migration.

The terraform state mv command is the key to state migration in Terraform. This command allows you to move resources within a state or between states, effectively changing the resource address recorded in the state. Let us look at an example of migrating an Azure virtual machine (azurerm_virtual_machine.example) from a module (module.old) to the root module:

```
terraform state mv module.old.azurerm_virtual_machine.example
azurerm_virtual_machine.example
```

This command tells Terraform to change the address of the specified resource in the state, avoiding the need to destroy and recreate the resource in the process. Please note that you should revise the Terraform configurations to reflect the address change before running terraform apply again.

When it comes to migrating state between backends, you first need to initialize the new backend with terraform init and specify the new backend configuration. When prompted by Terraform, agree to copy the state to the new backend:

```
terraform init -backend-config="new-backend.hcl"

# Terraform will ask for the confirmation to copy state to the new backend

Do you want to copy existing state to the new backend?
  Pre-existing state was found while migrating the previous "local" backend to the
  newly configured "azurerm" backend. No existing state was found in the newly
  configured "azurerm" backend. Do you want to copy this state to the new
"azurerm"
```

backend? Enter "yes" to copy and "no" to start with an empty state.

Enter a value: yes

Remember to handle state migration carefully, as incorrect state manipulations can lead to lost or inconsistent infrastructure state. As a best practice, always back up the state before performing state migrations and test the process in a non-production environment if possible. With appropriate planning and execution, state migration can help you adapt the Terraform management to evolving infrastructure needs and practices.

# Summary

In this chapter, we dove into the concept of Terraform state, which is an essential part of how Terraform manages and tracks the infrastructure. We learned that the state file maintains a record of the resources Terraform has created, thus allowing it to keep the infrastructure and configuration in sync. It keeps a record of IDs, properties, and metadata, all of which Terraform uses to map its resources to real-world resources.

We also explored local and remote states, comparing the two to better understand their functionality and use cases. Local state is a simple JSON file stored locally, whereas remote state involves storing the state file on a remote backend like Azure Blob Storage or HashiCorp's Terraform Cloud. Remote state offers advantages like enhanced security, state sharing and locking mechanisms that prevent state corruption during concurrent operations.

We then shifted our focus to state manipulation, understanding how to perform it and its implications. Through practical examples, we got a taste of how to use the terraform state mv command to move and rename resources, which allows us to refactor our Terraform configurations without affecting the actual infrastructure. We also explored potential state conflicts and learned to resolve them using the state command.

Lastly, we delved into state drift, reconciliation, and migration. We learned how changes in infrastructure outside of Terraform can cause drift from the state file. By running the terraform refresh command, we can update the state file to match the real infrastructure, essentially reconciling state drift. For state migration, we saw how to use terraform state mv to change the resource address in the state, and how to transfer the state to a new backend using terraform init with a new backend configuration. We realized the importance of careful state migration to avoid losing or corrupting the infrastructure state.

# CHAPTER 6:
# PROVISIONERS AND
# PROVISIONING
# RESOURCES

# Introduction to Infrastructure Provisioning

## Overview

Provisioning in IT is the act of establishing a functional IT framework. It requires the completion of a wide variety of tasks, including the installation and configuration of software, the setting up of both physical and virtual servers, the management of storage, the configuration of networks, and more. Provisioning is now commonly used to refer to the process of setting up infrastructure in a cloud environment, such as AWS, Google Cloud, or Azure. This is because cloud computing has become increasingly popular. Provisioning is a process that is used to get the infrastructure ready for use in a way that is dependable, automated, and repeatable. This procedure is necessary in order to guarantee that the infrastructure will be set up appropriately and in a consistent manner. It shortens the time it takes to deploy new features while simultaneously cutting the amount of time spent offline due to faults and inconsistencies in configuration settings. Businesses are able to scale their infrastructure to match demand through the use of provisioning, which ensures that they only pay for what they use at the time that they require it. Provisioning can be carried out programmatically in the case of cloud-based infrastructure by making use of technologies that treat infrastructure as code, such as Terraform.

Moving on to the topic of resource provisioning, this term describes the process by which a cloud provider allots their available resources and services to an individual user's account. In a broader sense, the phrase can also refer to any configuration of those resources that is required following the provisioning of such resources in order to make them available for use. In a cloud environment, some resources that can be provisioned include virtual machines (VMs), databases, storage buckets, network interfaces, load balancers, and so on. Other examples of resources that can be provisioned include load balancers and so on.

Using the HashiCorp Configuration Language (HCL), Terraform, which is a resource provisioning tool, gives you the ability to write descriptions of these resources and their configurations in a language that is legible by humans. This language is uncomplicated and simple to grasp, and it enables you to represent cloud architecture in a way that can be versioned and reviewed in the same manner as any other code.

## Advantages of Resource Provisioning

Automating infrastructure provisioning with Terraform provides several compelling benefits:

### *Automated, Repeatable Deployments*

Defining infrastructure as code allows the same components to be deployed consistently and repeatedly across environments. Instead of manual setup, Terraform automates deployment based on the configurations. This reduces human errors and instills confidence that environments will be identical every time. Teams can rapidly rebuild infrastructure for testing or development workflows.

## Facilitated Change Management

With infrastructure codified, changes can be managed through version control systems like Git. All modifications are reviewed, tracked, and audited in the git history. Engineers can easily roll back to previous versions if issues arise. Complex change management becomes simplified through mature version control practices.

## Lower Operational Costs

By reducing manual operations and customizing infrastructure programmatically, Terraform drives significant operational efficiency. Time spent on mundane configuration and setup is replaced by automated deployment. Operational costs decrease as infrastructure scales.

## Flexible Scalability

Scaling infrastructure capacity up or down can be achieved by modifying resource counts and properties in the Terraform code. What once required extensive manual effort to scale can now be accomplished through trivial code changes. Infrastructure becomes flexible and responsive to evolving demands.

## Consistent Environments

Terraform facilitates keeping development, testing, and production environments identical. The same configurations deploy to each environment, eliminating configuration drift. This consistency streamlines testing and deployment by eliminating environment-specific bugs. Reliability improves as environments align.

In the following sections, we'll delve into how Terraform handles resource provisioning, and how to make the most out of its features and capabilities.

# Built-In Provisioners

Terraform has a concept called "provisioners" that are used as a last resort option to execute scripts or actions on the local machine or on a remote machine after the resource is created. They are generally used to bootstrap a system, alter default settings, or set up specific configurations that can't be set in the resource definition itself.

Provisioners can be used in conjunction with any resource. It is important to note that

Terraform designs these to run provisioners when the resource is first created. If a resource successfully creates but fails during provisioning, Terraform will mark the resource as "tainted", indicating that it exists but failed to fully set up. The next terraform apply command will destroy and recreate the resource if it's tainted, hoping to establish a fully functioning resource.

Terraform has several built-in provisioners:

- File Provisioner: This provisioner is used to copy files or directories from the machine executing Terraform to newly created resources. The file provisioner is also able to upload directories. When uploading a directory, it can be useful to use file permissions that allow the destination files to be overwritten.

- Local-exec Provisioner: This invokes a local executable after a resource is created. This is a great way to kick off a configuration management tool, bootstrap into a cluster, etc. The local-exec provisioner does not retry and does not wait for success, so if it fails, so does the provisioner.

- Remote-exec Provisioner: This invokes a script on a remote resource after it is created. This can be used to run a configuration management tool, bootstrap into a cluster, or even notify a REST API with the IP address and other details of the resource.

- Null Resource Provisioner: This is a unique type of resource that does not interact with any external system, but instead allows managing the higher-level behavior of Terraform itself. Null resources and the triggers argument allow you to create dependencies for items Terraform doesn't automatically infer, or cause a set of actions to be taken based on changes elsewhere.

While provisioners can be handy in some situations, they also have limitations and can lead to hard-to-debug, unreliable, or hard-to-update configurations. For instance, they are only run at resource creation time, leaving you on the own when updating or deleting resources. Also, errors in provisioners lead to tainted resources, forcing you to recreate the resource if a provisioner fails.

As a result, HashiCorp recommends using provisioners as a last resort. It's often better to solve the problem using other methods if possible, such as directly configuring the needed settings via the Terraform resource, using cloud-init or similar tools for instance configuration, or employing a separate configuration management tool like Ansible or Chef.

In the following sections, we will go over examples of using these built-in provisioners and how to handle their peculiarities and edge cases.

## File Provisioner

The file provisioner in Terraform is a great tool for copying files or directories from the local machine to newly created resources, such as virtual machines. To use the file provisioner, you will need to specify the source and destination of the files or directories you wish to copy.

Let us consider an example where you have created a virtual machine in Azure and want to copy a script file to the home directory of the default user. The script could be a bash script that configures the VM after creation or runs some initial setup commands.

Following is a sample program on how you could do that:

```
resource "azurerm_virtual_machine" "vm" {
  name               = "vm-example"
  location           = "West Europe"
  resource_group_name = "resource-group-example"
  network_interface_id = "${azurerm_network_interface.example.id}"
  vm_size            = "Standard_A0"

  delete_os_disk_on_termination = true
  delete_data_disks_on_termination = true

  storage_image_reference {
    publisher = "Canonical"
    offer    = "UbuntuServer"
    sku      = "16.04-LTS"
    version  = "latest"
  }

  os_profile {
    computer_name  = "vmexample"
    admin_username = "adminuser"
```

```
  admin_password = "Password1234!"
}

os_profile_linux_config {
  disable_password_authentication = false
}

provisioner "file" {
  source      = "setup.sh"
  destination = "/home/adminuser/setup.sh"

  connection {
    type     = "ssh"
    user     = "adminuser"
    password = "Password1234!"
    host     = "${azurerm_public_ip.example.ip_address}"
  }
}
}
```

In the above given program, Terraform is creating an Azure VM using the "azurerm_virtual_machine" resource. After the VM is created, the "file" provisioner is triggered. It uploads a file called "setup.sh" from the local machine to the "/home/adminuser" directory on the VM. The connection block describes how Terraform should connect to the instance to execute the provisioner. This is done over SSH, connecting to the public IP address assigned to the instance.

Keep in mind that you need to replace the "Password1234!" and "${azurerm_public_ip.example.ip_address}" with the actual VM password and IP address respectively.

The file provisioner is most commonly used with resources that create compute instances. However, it can be used with any resource that has a connection block defined. This provisioner can also be used in conjunction with others to fully automate the resource setup process. For example, after copying a script file to a newly created instance, you can use the "remote-exec" provisioner to execute that script.

# Local-exec Provisioner

The local-exec provisioner invokes a local command after a resource is created. This provisioner does not require any kind of connectivity to the resource it operates on - it executes the command on the machine where Terraform is run. The command is invoked directly through the system shell, which means it has access to system environment variables, and can make use of standard I/O channels for interactivity.

Let us take the case where you need to create a resource (an Azure storage account, for instance) and after its creation, you want to run a local script that will add some initial data to the storage account. Below is an example of how you can achieve this:

```
resource "azurerm_storage_account" "example" {
  name                     = "example"
  resource_group_name      = azurerm_resource_group.example.name
  location                 = azurerm_resource_group.example.location
  account_tier             = "Standard"
  account_replication_type = "GRS"

  provisioner "local-exec" {
    command = "./populate_storage.sh ${self.primary_access_key}"
  }
}
```

In the example above, we are creating a new Azure storage account. After the creation of the storage account, the local-exec provisioner runs a local script called populate_storage.sh. The ${self.primary_access_key} variable is an attribute of the azurerm_storage_account resource that gives us the access key of the storage account. This access key is passed as an argument to the populate_storage.sh script, which presumably uses it to authenticate with the Azure storage account and populate it with data.

The local-exec provisioner is incredibly versatile and can be used to call APIs, trigger other tools, send notifications, or perform housekeeping tasks like logging or cleanup.

One crucial thing to remember with local provisioners is that they only run when the resource they are defined within is created. If the resource is later updated or destroyed, the local provisioner will not be re-run unless the resource is recreated.

Also, remember that the script being called (populate_storage.sh in our case) needs to be executable and properly handle any arguments that you're passing to it. If there are any errors in the script, it could cause the Terraform run to fail.

Finally, remember that local-exec provisioners can introduce a dependence on local state, making the Terraform configuration less portable. Avoid relying on local shell scripts whenever possible, and aim for the Terraform configurations to be self-contained.

Next, we'll look at another important provisioner type, remote-exec, which runs commands on the remote resource itself.

## Remote-exec Provisioner

The remote-exec provisioner allows you to execute commands on a remote resource after it's created. This can be used to perform a wide range of tasks, such as installing software, changing settings, or simply testing that the resource is working as expected.

Let us consider a scenario where you want to create a new Azure virtual machine and then run a shell script on that virtual machine after it's created. Below is a sample program of how you might achieve this using the remote-exec provisioner:

```
resource "azurerm_virtual_machine" "example" {
  name                = "example"
  location            = "West US"
  resource_group_name = azurerm_resource_group.example.name
  network_interface_id = azurerm_network_interface.example.id
  vm_size             = "Standard_D2s_v3"

  storage_image_reference {
    publisher = "Canonical"
    offer     = "UbuntuServer"
    sku       = "16.04-LTS"
    version   = "latest"
  }

  os_profile {
    computer_name  = "hostname"
```

```
    admin_username = "admin"
  }

  os_profile_linux_config {
    disable_password_authentication = true
    ssh_keys {
      path    = "/home/admin/.ssh/authorized_keys"
      key_data = file("~/.ssh/id_rsa.pub")
    }
  }

  provisioner "remote-exec" {
    inline = [
      "sudo apt-get update",
      "sudo apt-get install -y nginx",
    ]
  }
}
```

In the above given program, after the virtual machine is created, the remote-exec provisioner runs a series of commands on the virtual machine. These commands update the package manager and then install the nginx web server.

The remote-exec provisioner requires some form of connectivity to the resource. In this case, it's using SSH, which is configured in the os_profile_linux_config block of the azurerm_virtual_machine resource. The SSH keys used are those from the local machine where Terraform is being run (assumed to be ~/.ssh/id_rsa.pub).

The commands executed by the remote-exec provisioner are defined in the inline argument. These commands are run in the order they are listed.

Similar to the local-exec provisioner, the remote-exec provisioner only runs when the resource is created. If the resource is later updated or destroyed, the remote-exec provisioner won't be re-run unless the resource is recreated.

Take note, while powerful, provisioners can lead to configurations that are hard to maintain and evolve. They can also create difficulties in destroying resources, because the provisioner configuration might rely on the existence of resources that are destroyed concurrently. Therefore, it's advised to use provisioners as a last resort when specific tooling for the system you're interacting with doesn't exist yet or when native Terraform resource types do not support the functionality you need.

# Null Resource Provisioner

The null_resource is a unique resource in Terraform's arsenal. While most resources correspond to some sort of infrastructure object, the null_resource does not. Instead, it is often combined with provisioners to perform arbitrary actions.

A null_resource could be used in several scenarios where some operation needs to be performed that isn't tied directly to the lifecycle of an actual resource. One common usage is when a provisioner must run every time Terraform runs, or based on some other resource changing.

A simplified example of a null_resource with a local-exec provisioner is:

```
resource "null_resource" "example" {
 provisioner "local-exec" {
   command = "echo 'This will always run'"
 }

 triggers = {
   always_run = "${timestamp()}"
 }
}
```

In this case, the provisioner within the null_resource will execute its actions every time Terraform runs because the triggers attribute is keyed to the current time, which changes on every run.

Now, let us consider a practical example. Suppose we have a web server for which Terraform is managing configuration, but we need to notify a chat room anytime the server configuration changes:

```
resource "null_resource" "chat_notification" {
```

```
triggers = {
  server_config = azurerm_virtual_machine.example.id
}

provisioner "local-exec" {
  command = "curl -X POST -H 'Content-type: application/json' --data
'{\"text\":\"Server configuration changed. ID:
${azurerm_virtual_machine.example.id}\"}'
https://hooks.slack.com/services/EXAMPLE/EXAMPLE/EXAMPLE"
  }
}
```

In the above given program, we're using the local-exec provisioner to send a message to a Slack channel when the azurerm_virtual_machine resource changes. The triggers attribute is observing the id of azurerm_virtual_machine.example resource. When that id changes, it means the server has been recreated, and it will re-run the provisioner to send a new message.

These examples demonstrate the power and flexibility of null_resource. However, keep in mind that its use should be limited. The null_resource is a procedural construct in the declarative Terraform language. Overuse of the null_resource could lead to complex and confusing Terraform configurations. It should be used as a last resort when there's no other more declarative options available. Always strive to use native Terraform resources and data sources when possible.

# Using Provisioners for Configuration Management

Config management is one of the pivotal aspects of infrastructure management that ensures that systems are in their desired states. With the evolution of IaC tools like Terraform, managing configurations has become more streamlined and efficient. Using provisioners with Terraform can provide you with the power to do much more than just creating and managing infrastructure. Let us proceed to delve into how provisioners are used for config management.

Provisioners in Terraform can be used to model specific actions on the local machine or on a remote machine in order to prepare servers or other infrastructure objects for service.

However, it is important to note that while provisioners can be used to handle certain parts of configuration management, they are not a full-fledged configuration management solution like Puppet, Chef, or Ansible.

Let us take an example scenario where we are deploying a web server on an Azure VM. In this case, you can use the remote-exec provisioner to install necessary software after the VM is created but before it's put into service.

```
resource "azurerm_virtual_machine" "web" {
  ...
  provisioner "remote-exec" {
   inline = [
     "sudo apt-get update",
     "sudo apt-get install -y nginx"
   ]
  }
}
```

In the example above, we're using the remote-exec provisioner to execute commands on the VM after it's created. This helps to ensure that the software is installed as part of the creation process of the VM.

However, it's worth noting that using provisioners as the primary means for software configuration has its downsides. Terraform is excellent at creating, managing, and combining cloud resources, but it's not designed to replace configuration management tools that are optimized for software configuration. Provisioners only run at resource creation time. If you need ongoing system management, you should use a dedicated configuration management tool or service.

As an alternative, you can use provisioners to bootstrap a more comprehensive configuration management solution. For example, you could use the remote-exec provisioner to install and start a configuration management agent like Puppet, Chef, or Ansible. Then, that agent can take over for further configuration tasks.

```
resource "azurerm_virtual_machine" "web" {
  ...
  provisioner "remote-exec" {
```

```
  inline = [
    "curl -O https://example.com/setup-ansible.sh",
    "chmod +x setup-ansible.sh",
    "./setup-ansible.sh"
  ]
 }
}
```

In the above given syntaxes, a script (setup-ansible.sh) is downloaded from a server and executed. The script can then install Ansible, pull down a playbook, and execute it. This enables Ansible to manage the system's state from that point onward.

Using provisioners for config management provides flexibility, but remember it's a stopgap measure for specific use-cases and not meant to replace full-fledged config management tools. A robust strategy often involves Terraform for infrastructure management and tools like Puppet, Chef, Ansible for configuration management. Terraform gets the infrastructure set up, and then these tools ensure the systems are correctly and consistently configured.

# Provisioning Errors

In the world of Infrastructure as Code (IaC), the introduction of errors during the provisioning phase can have significant consequences. Terraform provides a means to handle such errors, allowing developers to navigate around the pitfalls that may arise.

## Scripting Errors

One of the most common errors that occur with provisioners is errors in the scripts being executed. If the script has any syntax errors or it tries to perform an operation that fails, the Terraform apply operation will also fail.

*Solution*

Always test the scripts independently before integrating them with the Terraform code. Make sure that the commands are suitable for the target system (e.g., correct package manager for the OS), that any paths are correct, and that any dependencies of the script are met.

## Connection Errors

Terraform requires connectivity to the target system in order to execute provisioners like remote-exec. Connection issues could be due to networking issues, incorrect credentials, or a system not being ready for connections.

*Solution*
Validate the network access, credentials, and consider using the depends_on argument to ensure that any necessary network resources are created before the provisioner is run. Also, consider using the remote-exec provisioner's inline argument to add a delay or a wait for network readiness on the system.

# Idempotency Errors

Unlike Terraform's core resource model, provisioners are not idempotent. Running them multiple times can have different results. For example, a provisioner might attempt to install software that's already installed or attempt to start a service that's already running.

*Solution*
Design the provisioner scripts to be idempotent, i.e., they can be safely run multiple times and achieve the same result. This could be achieved by checking for the existence of a file before trying to create it, or checking the status of a service before attempting to start it.

# Timeout Errors

By default, Terraform will wait for up to 5 minutes for a provisioner to complete. If the operation doesn't complete in that time, Terraform will consider it an error.

*Solution*
The default timeout can be adjusted using the timeouts block in the resource that the provisioner is associated with. Determine an appropriate timeout value based on what the provisioner is doing.

# Destruction Errors

Provisioners are also run when a resource is destroyed, which can lead to errors if the provisioner relies on something that has already been destroyed.

*Solution*
Use when = "create" to ensure that the provisioner only runs upon resource creation.

# Resource Does Not Yet Exist

This error typically occurs when Terraform attempts to run a provisioner before the resource it is attached to has been fully created.

*Solution*
Make use of the depends_on argument to specify resource dependencies and control the order of resource creation.

Remember, error handling in Terraform requires a combination of careful script creation, thorough testing, and understanding the intricacies of how Terraform interacts with the resources.

# Terraform Provisioning Best Practices

Working with Terraform provisioners can seem challenging, but adhering to a set of best practices can make the experience smoother and more efficient. Following are some guidelines to follow:

## Limited Usage of Provisioners

As a general rule of thumb, use provisioners sparingly. This is because provisioners introduce a potential point of failure into the Terraform configuration. Instead, opt for cloud-init or other cloud-specific initialization systems whenever possible. Try to encapsulate this within the instances by using startup scripts or utilizing a configuration management tool.

## Idempotent Scripts

When writing provisioner scripts, it's important to design them to be idempotent. In the context of provisioners, idempotency means that the scripts can be safely run multiple times without causing unintended side effects. For instance, instead of writing a script that simply starts a service, you might write a script that first checks whether the service is already running and then starts it only if necessary. This makes the script safe to run even if the service is already running, thereby ensuring that the script behaves predictably and consistently.

## Explicit Dependencies

Another important consideration when using provisioners is to explicitly specify dependencies between resources and provisioners using the depends_on argument. This can help to ensure that operations are performed in the correct order. For example, you might use depends_on to ensure that a database instance is fully created before a provisioner attempts to initialize the database. This can help to prevent timing issues or errors caused by attempts to modify resources that do not yet exist.

# Error Handling

Always include error handling in your provisioner scripts. If a command in a provisioner script fails, the script should handle that failure in a meaningful way, rather than simply causing the entire script to fail. This might involve logging an error message, retrying the operation, or performing some sort of cleanup or rollback operation. Including robust error handling in your provisioner scripts can make your infrastructure provisioning process more robust and resilient, and it can help to prevent minor issues from causing major disruptions.

# Using 'Self' in Connection Blocks

When referring to attributes of the resource to which a provisioner is assigned, use the self object. This makes it clear that you are referring to the associated resource, not some other resource that may have a similar name.

# Avoid Inline Provisioning Scripts

Rather than incorporating lengthy inline scripts directly within your Terraform code, it's advisable to place these scripts in separate files and employ Terraform's 'file' function to import them. This approach contributes to maintaining a clean and organized Terraform codebase. Additionally, it facilitates the reuse of scripts across multiple resources and simplifies the process of independently testing these scripts, thereby enhancing overall code quality and maintainability.

# Secure Connections

First and foremost, always secure your connections. When using remote-exec provisioners, it's recommended to secure the connection using SSH keys instead of passwords. SSH keys provide a more secure method of logging into a virtual private server with SSH than using a password alone. With SSH keys, a private and public key pair are created, the private key remains on your local machine and should be kept secure, while the public key is added onto the server. This method ensures that the server will only be accessible to machines that possess the corresponding private key. This approach is not only more secure but also more reliable. If a password is forgotten, the only solution is to reset it. However, with SSH keys, as long as you don't lose your keys, you'll always have access to your servers.

# Retry Failed Provisioners

In the world of networked computing, intermittent issues are a fact of life. Connections drop, servers reboot, updates get applied, and sometimes things just break. When these things happen, your Terraform provisioners might fail. To handle such scenarios, you can use the null_resource with triggers to retry failed provisioners. This allows Terraform to attempt running the provisioners again when intermittent issues occur, increasing the reliability of your Terraform runs.

## Clean up with Destroy Provisioners

Provisioners are not only useful for setting up resources, but they can also be used when a resource is destroyed. This is particularly useful for cleanup tasks that need to be performed before a resource is deleted. For instance, you might need to remove a server from a load balancer pool before the server is destroyed, or you might need to deregister a machine from a configuration management system. To specify a destroy provisioner, use the "when = destroy" argument. This tells Terraform to run the provisioner when the resource is being destroyed.

## Test Provisioners Separately

Before integrating provisioner scripts into your Terraform code, it's a good idea to test them independently. This allows for any errors to be caught and rectified early in the development process, making the process smoother and more efficient. It also helps ensure that your Terraform runs don't fail due to issues with the provisioners.

## Document the Code

Last but certainly not least, always document your code. This is crucial for the maintainability of the code and aids in team collaboration. Good documentation should describe what the code does, why it does it, and how it does it. It should also include any important information about dependencies, assumptions, or requirements. This not only helps others understand and use your code, but it can also be a lifesaver when you come back to your code after a long absence. Remember, code is read much more often than it is written, so invest the time to make your code as clear as possible.

By following best practices like using cloud-init or configuration management tools, designing idempotent scripts, specifying explicit dependencies, and including robust error handling, you can use provisioners effectively while minimizing the potential for problems.

# Summary

In this chapter, we dove further into our understanding of Terraform provisioners to get the full picture. After gaining a concept of resource provisioning as a starting point, we discovered how it plays an essential role in the deployment of infrastructure by assisting in the configuration and startup of servers, apps, and other components. Because provisioning helps reduce manual setup, promotes consistency, and saves time, the efficiency with which infrastructure is deployed is considerably improved.

We took a more in-depth look at the many sorts of in-built provisioners that are available through Terraform, examining the specific use cases for each one as well as the steps to build it. This included the local-exec provisioner, which enables executing scripts locally on the system running Terraform, as well as the remote-exec provisioner, which enables running commands on the resource that is being created or changed. Additionally, this included the file provisioner, which copies files or directories to a destination location. We also went over the null resource provisioner, which is a one-of-a-kind piece of software that correlates provisioning activities with any arbitrary collection of adjustments. In addition, we investigated the best ways to use provisioners for administration of configuration settings. This included the various faults that can arise throughout the process as well as the methods that can be utilized to properly handle them. In addition to this, it emphasized how essential it is to adhere to industry standards in order to avoid any potential problems. Validating the configurations, properly handling failures, guaranteeing idempotency, and carefully managing dependencies were some of the guiding principles mentioned in these standards.

In the final section of this chapter, examples were given that demonstrated why employing provisioners isn't always the most effective approach. It emphasized the significance of utilizing provisioners wisely and warned against scenarios that had the potential to result in problems with either the infrastructure or the operations of the organization. This understanding will lead the process of decision-making, helping to establish which tools and tactics are the most successful for deploying and managing infrastructure.

# CHAPTER 7: WORKING WITH SECRETS

# Secrets Management Overview

As we navigate further into our Terraform learning journey, let us focus our attention on a topic that plays a pivotal role in securing any application or service - Secrets. In the context of IT infrastructure and software applications, secrets refer to any form of sensitive data which, if exposed, could lead to unauthorized access and potential data breaches. Secrets could be anything like API keys, database credentials, SSH keys, certificates, tokens, or any other piece of information that provides access to APIs, databases, or other services.

The importance of secrets management cannot be understated. It is a key element of modern infrastructure management and contributes to the overall security posture of an organization. Secrets are like the keys to the kingdom, and therefore, how you manage these keys can determine the safety of the kingdom. Poor management of secrets can lead to a data breach, negatively affecting a company's reputation, causing financial loss, and in some cases, even leading to legal consequences.

Secrets management involves the secure handling of confidential data like passwords, API keys, certificates, and encryption keys throughout their entire lifecycle. It encompasses creation, distribution, storage, rotation, and retirement of secrets. Robust secrets management is critical for several reasons:

- Enables compliance with data security regulations that mandate protection of sensitive information like personally identifiable data. Non-compliance results in legal and financial penalties.

- Safeguards against data breaches and unauthorized access. Compromised secrets can lead to account takeovers, data exfiltration, service disruptions, and other incidents.

- Allows implementing automated, secure handling of credentials instead of hardcoding secrets in source code or configs. Automation reduces human error risks.

- Provides detailed audit trails tracking all access to secrets. This supports accountability and investigation if misuse is suspected.

- Facilitates periodic rotation of secrets to limit exposure over time, as well as rapid revocation if secrets become compromised.

- Centralizes storage and management of secrets under strict access controls instead of scattered credentials.

These points only touch the surface of why secrets management is vital in maintaining a secure, scalable, and resilient infrastructure. A robust secrets management strategy is no longer a luxury but a necessity in today's rapidly evolving digital landscape. It ensures the integrity of the IT infrastructure and helps build trust with the users, customers, and stakeholders. As we delve deeper into secrets management, we'll discuss some of the methods and tools that are commonly used in the industry.

# Process Flow of Secrets Management

As we unravel the world of secrets management, it is vital to understand the standard process flow that governs it. This process enables organizations to securely manage sensitive data throughout its lifecycle. The main steps involved in a typical secrets management process are as follows:

## Secret Creation

The lifecycle of a secret begins with its creation. This could be anything from an API token, a password, an SSH key, or a certificate. Secrets should be created in a secure manner, often involving algorithms for generating random and complex secrets that are difficult to crack. The goal here is to create robust, unique secrets that minimize the risk of being guessed or broken by brute force.

## Secret Storage

Once a secret is created, the next step is storing it securely. Secrets should never be stored in plain text or in easily accessible locations like code repositories or unencrypted databases. They should be stored in a dedicated and secure secrets management solution. These solutions offer encrypted storage, meaning even if someone gains access to the storage system, they can't read the secrets without the encryption key.

## Secret Access

Access to secrets should be strictly controlled and should follow the principle of least privilege (PoLP). This means that a user or service should only have access to the secrets required for its legitimate purpose, and no more. Fine-grained access controls and robust policies should be used to enforce this. Access to secrets should also be authenticated and authorized securely, often involving multiple factors of authentication.

## Secret Distribution

Secrets need to be distributed to the applications, services, or users that need them. This should be done in a secure way to ensure the secret does not get exposed in transit. This often involves using secure communication channels and protocols, for example, HTTPS or mutual TLS.

# Secret Rotation

Secrets should not remain static or long-lived. They should be rotated periodically, meaning new secrets are generated and the old ones retired. This minimizes the potential damage if a secret is exposed, as the exposed secret will only be valid for a limited time. Rotation should be automated as much as possible, to ensure it happens regularly and without requiring manual intervention.

# Secret Auditing

All access to secrets and changes to them should be logged and monitored. This helps in identifying any suspicious activity and provides an audit trail for investigation if a breach occurs. The audit logs themselves should be secured, as they can provide valuable information to an attacker.

# Secret Revocation and Retirement

If a secret is believed to be compromised or is no longer needed, it should be immediately revoked and retired. This means it can no longer be used to gain access. If a secret is compromised, an investigation should follow to determine how the breach occurred and to prevent it from happening again.

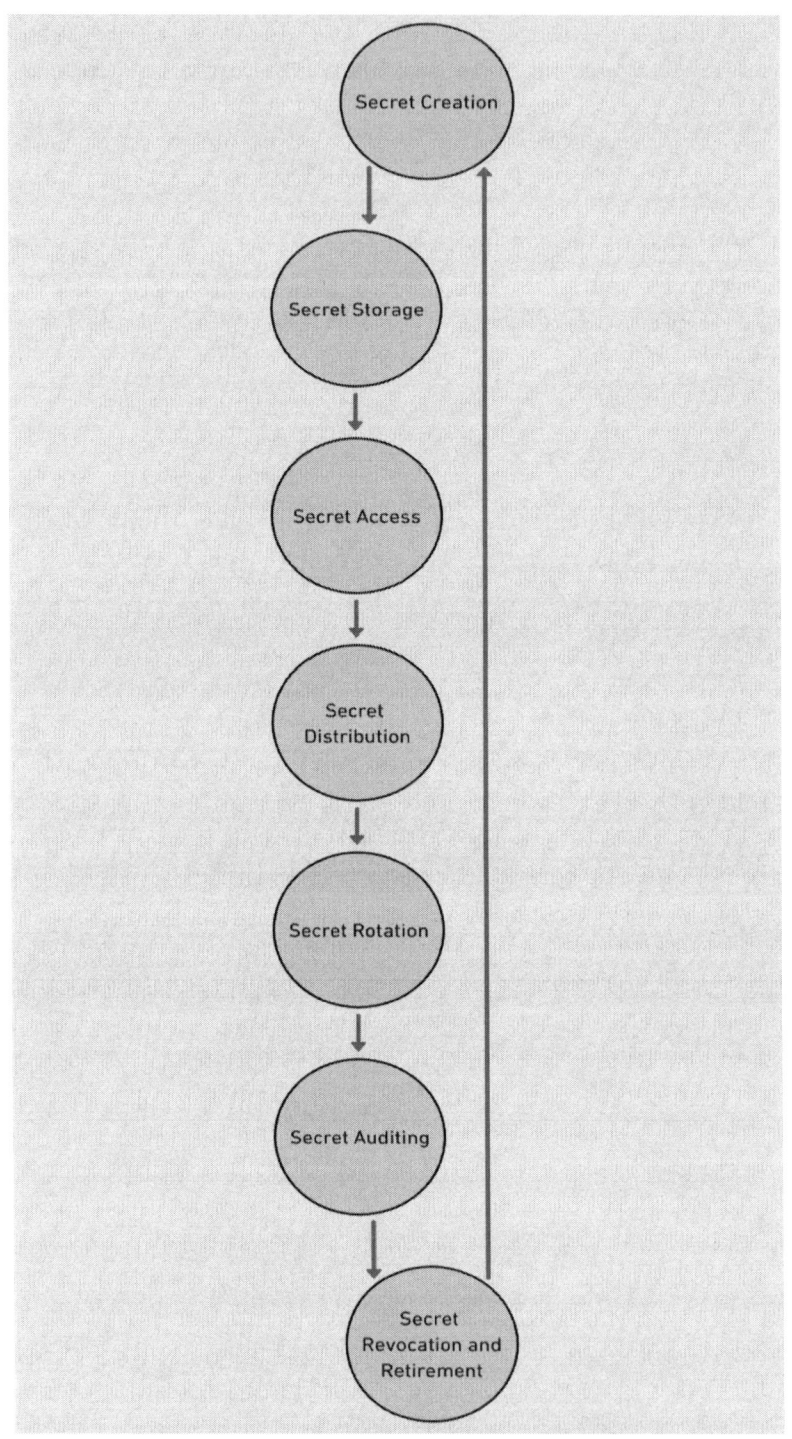

**Fig 7.1 Process of Secrets Management**

These seven steps form the backbone of a robust secrets management process. However, the specifics of each step can vary depending on the organization's needs and the specific tools used for secret management. Throughout these steps, it is crucial to remember the overarching aim of secrets management - to protect sensitive data from unauthorized access, thus maintaining the security and integrity of the organization's systems and data.

# Exploring Azure Key Vault

## Overview

Azure Key Vault is a service provided by Microsoft Azure to manage cryptographic keys, certificates, and secrets in a centralized cloud service, and control their distribution. Azure Key Vault is designed to handle three types of items:

Keys: Cryptographic keys used for encryption, decryption, or signing data.
Secrets: Sensitive information like database connection strings, passwords, and more.
Certificates: Public and private SSL/TLS certificates.

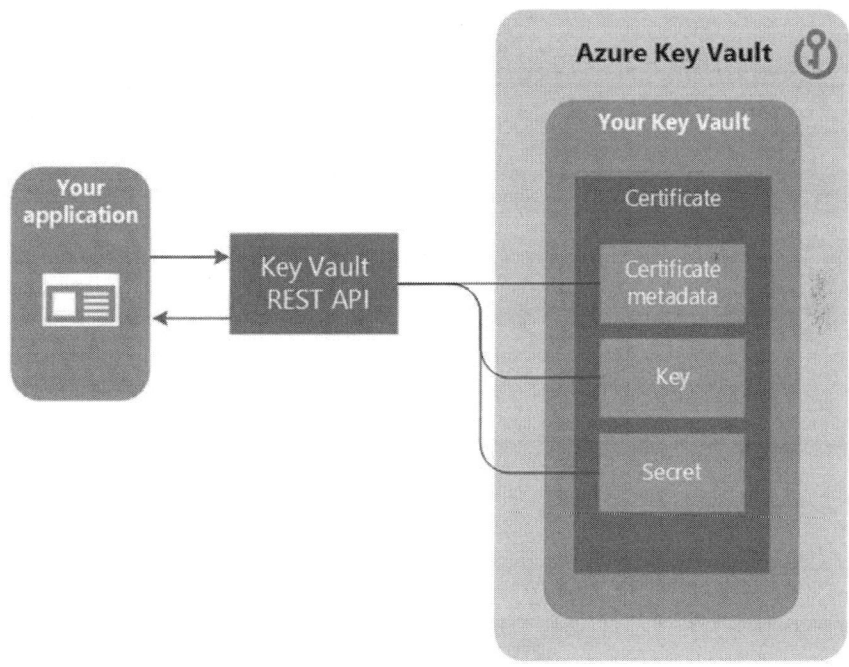

**Fig 7.2 Microsoft Azure Key Vault**

Azure Key Vault allows applications to securely store and tightly control access to these keys, secrets, and certificates, making it a vital tool for secrets management. Let us proceed to look at its capabilities and how to set it up within a Terraform environment.

## Capabilities of Azure Key Vault

Secure Storage: Azure Key Vault provides a secure location to store and manage secrets. The data is secured using hardware security modules (HSMs) that are compliant with FIPS 140-2 Level 2 and Common Criteria EAL4+.

- Access Control: Fine-grained access policies can be applied, allowing only authorized users and applications to retrieve the secrets.

- Audit Logs: Azure Key Vault tracks and logs all interactions, making it possible to monitor who is accessing which secrets and when.

- Automated Lifecycle Management: We can set expiration dates on secrets and keys and automate the process of rotating, expiring, and archiving them.

- Integration with Other Azure Services: Azure Key Vault can be integrated with various Azure services for managing and maintaining keys, secrets, and certificates used by them.

## Setting up Azure Key Vault in Terraform

Firstly, you will need to create a resource block for Azure Key Vault in the Terraform configuration file. This block will provide the configuration for the Azure Key Vault service. Following is an example:

```
resource "azurerm_key_vault" "example" {
  name                        = "examplekeyvault"
  location                    = azurerm_resource_group.example.location
  resource_group_name         = azurerm_resource_group.example.name
  enabled_for_disk_encryption = true
  tenant_id                   = data.azurerm_client_config.current.tenant_id
  soft_delete_retention_days  = 7
  purge_protection_enabled    = false

  sku_name = "standard"
```

```
}
```

This creates a Key Vault within a specified Azure resource group. The tenant_id parameter specifies the Azure Active Directory tenant ID that should be used for authenticating requests to the key vault.

Next, you need to add an access policy for the Azure Key Vault. The access policy will determine who has what kind of access to the Key Vault:

```
resource "azurerm_key_vault_access_policy" "example" {
  key_vault_id = azurerm_key_vault.example.id

  tenant_id = data.azurerm_client_config.current.tenant_id
  object_id = data.azurerm_client_config.current.object_id

  key_permissions = [
    "get",
  ]

  secret_permissions = [
    "get",
    "delete",
    "set",
  ]
}
```

In the above demonstration, you're granting the permissions to get, set, and delete secrets from the Key Vault to the current Azure user.

Now, let us add a secret to the Key Vault:

```
resource "azurerm_key_vault_secret" "example" {
  name         = "example-secret"
  value        = "s3cr3t"
  key_vault_id = azurerm_key_vault.example.id
```

```
}
```

This block creates a secret with the name "example-secret" and the value "s3cr3t" within the Azure Key Vault.

With these blocks in the Terraform configuration, you should be able to successfully setup Azure Key Vault and manage secrets. Remember to replace all the example values with the real values.

After writing the Terraform configuration, you can initialize the Terraform workspace with terraform init, validate the configuration using terraform validate, generate and review the execution plan with terraform plan, and finally, apply the changes using terraform apply.

Lastly, to access the secrets stored in Azure Key Vault from the Terraform configurations, you can use the azurerm_key_vault_secret data source:

```
data "azurerm_key_vault_secret" "example" {
  name         = "example-secret"
  key_vault_id = azurerm_key_vault.example.id
}

output "secret_value" {
  value = data.azurerm_key_vault_secret.example.value
}
```

This will retrieve the value of the "example-secret" secret and output it.

# Sample Program to Manage Secrets using Terraform

For the purpose of this example, let us say we have an application that requires database credentials. These credentials are considered sensitive information and shouldn't be stored directly in the Terraform code. Instead, we're going to securely store them in Azure Key Vault and access them when needed.

First, we need to configure the Azure provider and set up the Azure Key Vault resource. Below is the code snippet of how to do that:

```
provider "azurerm" {
  features {}
}

data "azurerm_client_config" "current" {}

resource "azurerm_resource_group" "example" {
  name     = "example-resources"
  location = "West Europe"
}

resource "azurerm_key_vault" "example" {
  name                        = "examplekeyvault"
  location                    = azurerm_resource_group.example.location
  resource_group_name         = azurerm_resource_group.example.name
  enabled_for_disk_encryption = true
  tenant_id                   = data.azurerm_client_config.current.tenant_id
  soft_delete_retention_days  = 7
  purge_protection_enabled    = false
  sku_name                    = "standard"
}
```

In this snippet, we have set up the provider, retrieved the current client configuration, defined a resource group, and set up the Azure Key Vault. We have enabled soft delete and set the retention days to 7.

Next, we need to create access policies for the Key Vault:

```
resource "azurerm_key_vault_access_policy" "example" {
  key_vault_id = azurerm_key_vault.example.id

  tenant_id = data.azurerm_client_config.current.tenant_id
  object_id = data.azurerm_client_config.current.object_id
```

```
key_permissions = [
  "get",
  "list"
]

secret_permissions = [
  "get",
  "set",
  "delete",
  "list",
]
}
```

In the above demonstration, we have given the current client permissions to get, set, delete, and list the secrets.

Now, let us store the database credentials as secrets in Azure Key Vault:

```
resource "azurerm_key_vault_secret" "db_username" {
  name         = "db-username"
  value        = "myusername"
  key_vault_id = azurerm_key_vault.example.id
}

resource "azurerm_key_vault_secret" "db_password" {
  name         = "db-password"
  value        = "mypassword"
  key_vault_id = azurerm_key_vault.example.id
}
```

In this block, we're creating two secrets: db-username and db-password, and storing them in the Azure Key Vault.

Now, let us say we have a Terraform configuration for an Azure SQL Database. We can use the azurerm_key_vault_secret data source to access the secrets:

```
data "azurerm_key_vault_secret" "db_username" {
  name         = "db-username"
  key_vault_id = azurerm_key_vault.example.id
}

data "azurerm_key_vault_secret" "db_password" {
  name         = "db-password"
  key_vault_id = azurerm_key_vault.example.id
}

resource "azurerm_sql_server" "example" {
  name                         = "mysqlserver"
  resource_group_name          = azurerm_resource_group.example.name
  location                     = azurerm_resource_group.example.location
  version                      = "12.0"
  administrator_login          = data.azurerm_key_vault_secret.db_username.value
  administrator_login_password =
data.azurerm_key_vault_secret.db_password.value
}
```

In this block, we're retrieving the db-username and db-password secrets from the Azure Key Vault and using them to set up the SQL server.

Remember to replace all the example values with the real values. Also, to avoid sensitive data being output to the console, you might want to set the sensitive attribute to true in the output block.

This is a simplified example of how to use Azure Key Vault for secrets management in a Terraform environment. Depending on the use case, you might need to customize the configurations. For instance, if you have multiple environments (e.g., development, staging, production), you might need to create different Key Vaults or secrets for each environment.

# Monitor and Log Secrets Access

The ability to monitor and log access to secrets is vital for maintaining the security and integrity of the systems. Azure Key Vault integrates with Azure Monitor and Azure Log Analytics, offering you the ability to view logs and set up alerts based on specific conditions. This way, you can keep an eye on who is accessing the secrets and when they're doing it. With Terraform, you can manage and configure these settings programmatically.

To begin with, let us make sure that Azure Key Vault is configured to log events. We'll need to create a Diagnostic Setting for our Key Vault. In this setting, we'll specify that we want to send our logs to a Log Analytics workspace. Following is a sample program on how you can do that with Terraform:

```
resource "azurerm_log_analytics_workspace" "example" {
  name                = "exampleworkspace"
  location            = azurerm_resource_group.example.location
  resource_group_name = azurerm_resource_group.example.name
  sku                 = "PerGB2018"
  retention_in_days   = 30
}

resource "azurerm_monitor_diagnostic_setting" "example" {
  name                       = "example"
  target_resource_id         = azurerm_key_vault.example.id
  log_analytics_workspace_id = azurerm_log_analytics_workspace.example.id

  log {
    category = "AuditEvent"
    enabled  = true

    retention_policy {
      enabled = true
      days    = 7
    }
  }
}
```

```
metric {
  category = "AllMetrics"

  retention_policy {
    enabled = true
    days   = 7
  }
 }
}
```

In the above given program, we've created a Log Analytics workspace with a 30-day retention policy. We then created a Diagnostic Setting for our Key Vault to send "AuditEvent" logs and "AllMetrics" to the Log Analytics workspace with a 7-day retention policy.

The "AuditEvent" logs will capture any event related to the access and usage of the secrets, like the retrieval of a secret, while "AllMetrics" will capture performance metrics. Depending on the needs, you might want to adjust the categories and retention days.

With the logs in place, you can now use Azure Monitor to create alerts based on certain conditions. For example, you can create an alert when a secret is accessed more than a certain number of times within a specified period.

In addition, Azure also provides the Azure Key Vault Activity Log, which records any write operation (PUT, PATCH, DELETE) performed on the Key Vault. This is especially useful to detect unauthorized changes.

Once you have the logs and alerts configured, you'll be well equipped to monitor and respond to any unexpected or unauthorized access to the secrets. Always remember, secrets management is a continuous process that involves not just securing the secrets but also monitoring their usage and adapting the strategy based on changing requirements and threat scenarios.

# Summary

In this chapter, we delved into secrets management, an integral part of maintaining the security of any application. We started by understanding what secrets are, their importance in application architecture, and the need for effective secrets management. Secrets like API keys, database credentials, encryption keys etc., are critical as they grant privileged access to resources and systems. The significance of managing these secrets properly to prevent unauthorized access or misuse is paramount. We also examined the standard process flow of secrets management, highlighting the four crucial stages: generation, storage, access, and rotation.

Our exploration took us to Azure Key Vault, a robust tool provided by Microsoft Azure to securely store and manage secrets. The platform is designed to handle the storage, access, and rotation of secrets, and integrates well with other Azure services. We discussed the initial setup process in a Terraform environment, underscoring Azure Key Vault's importance as a centralized, secure, and tightly controlled storage system for secrets. The Key Vault protects the secrets through access policies and role-based access controls, ensuring that only authorized entities have access.

Finally, we learned how to leverage Azure Key Vault to manage secrets in a Terraform configuration, with practical demonstrations on how to store, retrieve, and manage secrets. The functionality of monitoring and logging secrets access in Azure Key Vault was also discussed. By integrating with Azure Monitor and Azure Log Analytics, we were able to view logs, set up alerts, and track secret access. We concluded with a detailed walkthrough of how to implement monitoring and logging using Terraform, enabling enhanced security and oversight of secret management.

# CHAPTER 8: ADMINISTERING NETWORKS WITH TERRAFORM

# Essentials of Networking for Terraform

In order to have a complete understanding of Terraform, one of the most important components that needs to be mastered is networking. When we talk about networking, we are referring to the act of connecting different parts of our infrastructure to one another in order to provide them the ability to communicate with one another. We are responsible for managing virtual private clouds (VPCs), as well as subnets, routes, and internet gateways. In order to use Terraform for infrastructure management efficiently, you absolutely need to have a solid understanding of networking fundamentals.

The Azure networking resources are a collection of many different networking services that enable us to connect, defend, and monitor the network infrastructure that is hosted in the cloud as well as that which is hosted on-premises. The Azure Virtual Network, abbreviated as VNet, serves as the primary constituent in Azure's private networking infrastructure. Many different kinds of Azure resources, such as Azure Virtual Machines (VM), are able to connect in a safe and secure manner with one another, as well as with the internet and on-premises networks, thanks to VNet. A Virtual Network, or VNet, is comparable to a conventional network that you would operate in your very own data center; however, it comes with the added advantages that come with using Azure's infrastructure, such as increased scalability, availability, and isolation.

It is essential to have a solid understanding of how to develop and manage these resources in Azure using Terraform. For instance, the azurerm_virtual_network resource can be used to build a VNet, and the azurerm_subnet resource can be used to create a subnet within that VNet. Both of these resources are part of the Azure Virtual Network. Virtual machines (VMs) are capable of having network interfaces (azurerm_network_interface) attached to them so that they can communicate with the network.

The concept of networking security groups is yet another important one. These are analogous to firewalls for the cloud. We are able to construct firewall rules with Azure by utilizing network security groups and application security groups. These rules restrict the traffic that is sent to resources. For the purposes of defining and managing these rules in Terraform, the azurerm_network_security_group and azurerm_network_security_rule resources are utilized.

After that, there is the Azure Load Balancer, which is yet another networking resource that Terraform is able to control. This guarantees that the applications will always be highly available and will operate at their full potential. In order to manage this, Terraform makes use of the azurerm_lb resource.

We can also use Azure Private Link within the context of private networking. This gives you the ability to access Azure services (such as Azure Storage and Azure Cosmos DB) as well as Azure hosted customer-owned or partner services through a private endpoint within the VNet. As we continue to explore networking using Terraform, we will become familiar with additional resources and ideas, such as network peering, virtual network gateways, express route circuits, and DNS zones. Every one of these components contributes significantly to the infrastructure by bolstering the applications' capacity for improved communication and safety.

# Manage VPCs using Terraform

Managing Virtual Private Clouds (VPCs), or as they are referred to in Azure, Virtual Networks (VNet), with Terraform involves a series of steps to create and configure the necessary resources for a secure, private network. This process is an integral part of setting up cloud infrastructure, as it provides a secure environment for your resources and services to communicate with each other.

## Creating Virtual Network

The first step in this process is creating the virtual network itself. This is essentially a representation of your own network in the cloud. It is a logical isolation of the Azure cloud dedicated to your subscription. We can fully control the IP address range, subnets, routing tables, network gateways and security settings within this network.

Following is a sample Terraform code to create a VNet:

```
resource "azurerm_resource_group" "example" {
  name     = "example-resources"
  location = "West Europe"
}

resource "azurerm_virtual_network" "example" {
  name                = "example-network"
  resource_group_name = azurerm_resource_group.example.name
  location            = azurerm_resource_group.example.location
  address_space       = ["10.0.0.0/16"]
}
```

In the above given codes, we create a resource group and then a virtual network. The virtual network is given an address space of "10.0.0.0/16".

# Create Subnets

The next step is to create subnets within this virtual network. Check out the following syntax:

```
resource "azurerm_subnet" "example" {
  name                 = "example-subnet"
  resource_group_name  = azurerm_resource_group.example.name
  virtual_network_name = azurerm_virtual_network.example.name
  address_prefixes     = ["10.0.1.0/24"]
}
```

This block creates a subnet within the existing virtual network. The subnet is given an address space of "10.0.1.0/24", which is a subset of the VNet's address space.

# Define Network Interface

Now that we have a subnet, we can create a network interface. A network interface represents a network interface card (NIC), and it can be associated with a virtual machine to enable it to communicate with the network:

```
resource "azurerm_network_interface" "example" {
  name                = "example-nic"
  location            = azurerm_resource_group.example.location
  resource_group_name = azurerm_resource_group.example.name

  ip_configuration {
    name                          = "internal"
    subnet_id                     = azurerm_subnet.example.id
    private_ip_address_allocation = "Dynamic"
  }
}
```

In this block, we create a network interface and associate it with the subnet we created earlier. We specify that the IP address should be dynamically allocated.

## Manage Network Security

We can also manage network security groups (NSGs) which control inbound and outbound rules for network traffic:

```
resource "azurerm_network_security_group" "example" {
  name                = "example-nsg"
  location            = azurerm_resource_group.example.location
  resource_group_name = azurerm_resource_group.example.name
}

resource "azurerm_network_security_rule" "example" {
  name                        = "SSH"
  priority                    = 1001
  direction                   = "Inbound"
  access                      = "Allow"
  protocol                    = "Tcp"
  source_port_range           = "*"
  destination_port_range      = "22"
  source_address_prefix       = "*"
  destination_address_prefix  = "*"
  network_security_group_name =
azurerm_network_security_group.example.name
  resource_group_name         = azurerm_resource_group.example.name
}
```

In the above given codes, a network security group and a network security rule are created. The rule allows inbound SSH access.

As you can see, Terraform allows you to manage the whole lifecycle of VNet in Azure. From creating VNets, to creating subnets within those VNets, to creating and managing network interfaces and security rules, Terraform has got you covered.

# Manage Subnets and Routing

Once you have established a Virtual Network or Virtual Private Cloud (VPC), the subsequent step is to manage the subnets within it and set up routing. For the purpose of this discussion, we will continue to use Azure as our cloud service provider.

## Managing Subnets

Subnets are subdivisions of your Virtual Network as explained in the previous section. They allow you to segment the network into smaller parts, which can be beneficial for organizational, security, and traffic management purposes. For instance, you might want to separate your application servers from your database servers, or you might want to isolate development environments from production environments.

In Terraform, you manage subnets using the azurerm_subnet resource. This resource allows you to define each subnet as a separate entity within your Terraform configuration. Each subnet you define must have a unique address range within the VNet, specified in CIDR notation.

Below is the code snippet of how you might define a subnet in Terraform:

```
resource "azurerm_subnet" "subnet1" {
  name               = "subnet1"
  resource_group_name  = azurerm_resource_group.example.name
  virtual_network_name = azurerm_virtual_network.example.name
  address_prefixes     = ["10.0.1.0/24"]
}

resource "azurerm_subnet" "subnet2" {
  name               = "subnet2"
  resource_group_name  = azurerm_resource_group.example.name
  virtual_network_name = azurerm_virtual_network.example.name
  address_prefixes     = ["10.0.2.0/24"]
}
```

In this code, we create two subnets, each with a different address space within the virtual network.

# Managing Routing

Indeed, in Azure, routing is maintained not only through Route Tables but also through individual route entries. The movement of data packets across your Virtual Network and beyond is governed by the coordinated efforts of these parts working together.

In Azure, a Route Table is a collection of rules that, together referred to as routes, establish travel lanes for network traffic. We are able to establish and manage a Route Table in Terraform with the use of the azurerm_route_table resource. We have the option of specifying whether or not traffic should be automatically routed to the system routes whenever you create a Route Table.

The following is an illustration of one possible way to define a Route Table in Terraform:

```
resource "azurerm_route_table" "example" {
  name             = "example-route-table"
  location         = azurerm_resource_group.example.location
  resource_group_name = azurerm_resource_group.example.name
}


resource "azurerm_route" "route1" {
  name               = "route1"
  resource_group_name   = azurerm_resource_group.example.name
  route_table_name      = azurerm_route_table.example.name
  address_prefix        = "0.0.0.0/0"
  next_hop_type         = "VirtualAppliance"
  next_hop_in_ip_address = "10.0.0.4"
}


resource "azurerm_subnet_route_table_association" "example" {
  subnet_id      = azurerm_subnet.subnet1.id
  route_table_id = azurerm_route_table.example.id
}
```

In the above given demonstration, we create a route table, a route within that table, and associate it with our subnet1. The route table will direct all traffic (0.0.0.0/0) through a virtual appliance located at 10.0.0.4. We can create complex networks with multiple subnets and detailed routing rules, all in a repeatable, reliable way.

# Manage DNS

Terraform provides various resources to manage Domain Name System (DNS) settings. DNS is a critical part of any internet-facing infrastructure and managing it via code adds efficiency, flexibility, and reduces manual errors. Let us proceed to continue with our Azure examples.

The Azure Provider in Terraform provides DNS resources like azurerm_dns_zone to manage a DNS zone and azurerm_dns_a_record to manage A records within a zone.

Firstly, we can create a DNS Zone using the azurerm_dns_zone resource:

```
resource "azurerm_dns_zone" "example" {
  name                = "example.com"
  resource_group_name = azurerm_resource_group.example.name
  tags = {
    Environment = "Production"
  }
}
```

In this code, we create a DNS Zone for the domain example.com and tag it as "Production".

Next, we can create an A record that points to an IP address within this zone. Let us assume we have a public IP resource called azurerm_public_ip.example:

```
resource "azurerm_dns_a_record" "example" {
  name                = "www"
  zone_name           = azurerm_dns_zone.example.name
  resource_group_name = azurerm_resource_group.example.name
  ttl                 = 300
  records             = [azurerm_public_ip.example.ip_address]
}
```

In the above demonstration, we create an A record that points www.example.com to the IP address of our azurerm_public_ip.example resource. The TTL (Time to Live) is set to 300 seconds, meaning DNS servers will cache this record for up to 5 minutes.

Other DNS record types can be managed in a similar manner with other resources like azurerm_dns_cname_record for CNAME records and azurerm_dns_txt_record for TXT records.

Additionally, if you have a private DNS Zone in Azure, you can link it to the virtual network using the azurerm_private_dns_zone_virtual_network_link resource:

```
resource "azurerm_private_dns_zone_virtual_network_link" "example" {
  name                  = "example"
  resource_group_name   = azurerm_resource_group.example.name
  private_dns_zone_name = azurerm_private_dns_zone.example.name
  virtual_network_id    = azurerm_virtual_network.example.id
}
```

Managing DNS through Terraform brings all the benefits of Infrastructure as Code (IaC) - versioning, repeatability, and testing to another important part of the infrastructure. By defining these settings in code, you ensure that the DNS configuration is consistently applied, easily updated, and automatically documented. It also aligns the management of the DNS settings with the rest of the infrastructure.

# Manage Load Balancers

Managing load balancers and implementing automated scaling with Terraform can significantly improve the reliability and responsiveness of the applications. We'll use Azure as our cloud provider in the below sample codes.

A load balancer distributes network or application traffic across a number of servers. In Azure, you can create a load balancer using the azurerm_lb resource. Following is a simple example:

```
resource "azurerm_resource_group" "example" {
  name     = "example-resources"
  location = "West Europe"
}
```

```
resource "azurerm_public_ip" "example" {
  name             = "example-pip"
  location         = azurerm_resource_group.example.location
  resource_group_name = azurerm_resource_group.example.name
  allocation_method  = "Static"
}

resource "azurerm_lb" "example" {
  name             = "example-lb"
  location         = azurerm_resource_group.example.location
  resource_group_name = azurerm_resource_group.example.name

  frontend_ip_configuration {
    name             = "PublicIPAddress"
    public_ip_address_id = azurerm_public_ip.example.id
  }
}
```

In this code, we first create a resource group and a public IP address. We then create a load balancer and use the frontend_ip_configuration block to bind the public IP address to it.

Once the load balancer is ready, you can start adding rules for it. A rule defines how traffic is balanced. Below is the example of a load balancer rule:

```
resource "azurerm_lb_rule" "example" {
  resource_group_name            = azurerm_resource_group.example.name
  loadbalancer_id                = azurerm_lb.example.id
  name                           = "LBRule"
  protocol                       = "TCP"
  frontend_port                  = 80
  backend_port                   = 80
  frontend_ip_configuration_name = "PublicIPAddress"
```

```
}
```

In the above given example, we create a rule for the load balancer that listens on TCP port 80 and forwards traffic to the backend on the same port.

Now, let us talk about automated scaling. In Azure, you can achieve this using the azurerm_autoscale_setting resource.

```
resource "azurerm_autoscale_setting" "example" {
  name                = "example-autoscale"
  resource_group_name = azurerm_resource_group.example.name
  location            = azurerm_resource_group.example.location
  target_resource_id  = azurerm_virtual_machine_scale_set.example.id

  profile {
    name = "AutoScaleProfile"

    capacity {
      default = 1
      minimum = 1
      maximum = 5
    }

    rule {
      metric_trigger {
        metric_name        = "Percentage CPU"
        metric_resource_id = azurerm_virtual_machine_scale_set.example.id
        time_grain         = "PT1M"
        statistic          = "Average"
        time_window        = "PT5M"
        time_aggregation   = "Average"
        operator           = "GreaterThanOrEqual"
        threshold          = 75
      }
```

```
  scale_action {
    direction = "Increase"
    type     = "ChangeCount"
    value    = "1"
    cooldown = "PT5M"
   }
 }

 rule {
  metric_trigger {
    metric_name       = "Percentage CPU"
    metric_resource_id = azurerm_virtual_machine_scale_set.example.id
    time_grain        = "PT1M"
    statistic         = "Average"
    time_window       = "PT5M"
    time_aggregation  = "Average"
    operator          = "LessThanOrEqual"
    threshold         = 25
   }

  scale_action {
    direction = "Decrease"
    type     = "ChangeCount"
    value    = "1"
    cooldown = "PT5M"
   }
  }
 }
}
```

In the above given code sample, an autoscaling setting is created for a virtual machine scale set. Two rules are defined: one to increase the count of instances when the CPU usage is

75% or more, and another to decrease it when the usage is 25% or less. This ensures that the application can handle load peaks, but you don't overpay during quieter periods.

Terraform enables you to codify these elements of the infrastructure, allowing for replicability, version control, and easier changes. These practices ultimately lead to greater infrastructure resilience and efficiency.

# Network Configuration Troubleshooting

Terraform's error messages can be particularly helpful when debugging network configurations. Often, error messages will indicate missing required parameters, resources that could not be found, or values that were outside the allowed range.

Let us proceed to discuss a few common issues and solutions you might encounter while working with Terraform and network configurations:

## Missing Required Parameters

Many Terraform resources have required arguments that must be set for the resource to be created successfully. Omitting a required argument will lead to errors when trying to apply the configuration.

For example, creating an Azure network security group without specifying the location:

```
resource "azurerm_network_security_group" "example" {

  # Location is missing
}
```

Running apply would show an error:

```
Error: Missing required argument
```

### Solution

This occurs because the Azure provider requires the location argument when creating a network security group.

Fixing this issue involves:

- Checking provider documentation for which arguments are required
- Specifying all required arguments in the resource configuration
- Running validate and plan to catch missing arguments early

Required arguments act as mandatory settings that customize the resource. Common reasons for omitting required arguments are copy/pasting configs or incomplete knowledge of the resource arguments.

# Incorrect Reference to Other Resources

One common mistake when authoring Terraform configurations is attempting to reference a resource that has not been declared. For example, when defining an Azure subnet resource, we may accidentally misspell the name of the virtual network we want to attach it to:

```
resource "azurerm_subnet" "example" {
  virtual_network_name = azurerm_virtual_network.exampl.name
}
```

In the above snippet, we have a typo in the virtual network resource name ("exampl" instead of "example"). When applying this config, Terraform will raise an error:

```
Error: Resource not declared
```

## Solution

This error occurs because Terraform cannot find the resource being referenced since the name contains a mistake. The solution is to double check that all resource names referenced in the configuration match declared names exactly.

Common sources of this issue include:
- Misspelled resource names
- Forgetting to define a resource being referenced
- Accidentally referencing the wrong resource entirely

# Overlapping CIDR Blocks

Defining network resources like subnets or VPCs with overlapping CIDR blocks will lead to errors when provisioning the infrastructure.
For example, if two subnets within the same VPC are assigned address spaces that overlap:

```
resource "azurerm_subnet" "subnet1" {
  address_prefix = "10.0.0.0/16"
}

resource "azurerm_subnet" "subnet2" {
  address_prefix = "10.0.0.0/24"
}
```

The second subnet overlaps with the first. Applying this Terraform will fail with an error:

Error: CIDR blocks overlap

*Solution*
To resolve, the CIDR blocks must be disjoint. There are a few ways to achieve this:
- Adjust the prefixes to not overlap (e.g. 10.0.0.0/16 and 10.1.0.0/24)
- Create a variable for the VPC CIDR and derive non-overlapping subnet CIDRs
- Use the cidrsubnet() function to automatically partition VPC space
- Validate CIDRs don't overlap using validation tools like OPA

# Circular Dependencies

Sometimes, resources can be configured in a way that they depend on each other to be created. For instance, if an IAM policy requires a resource that depends on the IAM policy itself, Terraform will fail. Terraform will show an error like: Error creating IAM Role Policy Attachment: CircularDependency: Circular dependency between resources: [...]

*Solution*
To resolve, the chain of dependencies must be broken into a linear sequence without circular links. Ways to fix include:
- Separating the IAM policy into its own standalone resource
- Using the aws_iam_policy_document data source to build the policy doc
- Rearranging resources so dependencies flow in one direction
- Leveraging provisioners to apply policies after resource creation

By restructuring resources and policy attachments, we can eliminate the circular dependency. This provides Terraform a clear order in which to create interdependent components. Careful resource design is needed to anticipate and avoid circular chains. Checking dependency graphs helps reveal circular issues before applying. Resolving circular dependencies is key for successful Terraform usage.

In all of these cases, terraform validate and terraform plan are the friends. Run these commands before applying the changes to catch errors early. Don't forget to use terraform fmt and terraform taint to format the configuration and recreate resources, respectively. Be mindful that recreating resources could lead to downtime for production services.

# Summary

The first half of this chapter covered the foundations of networking in Terraform. In order to generate, manage, and update the infrastructure resources that are specified in the configuration file, Terraform makes use of the API provided by the provider. Virtual machines (VMs), databases, networks, and anything else can all be considered resources when working in the cloud. We have determined that infrastructure as code, often known as IaC, is an essential part of both the techniques and the ideas of DevOps. To define, deploy, and maintain the infrastructure, the plan is to build code and put it into operation. Declarative programming is the methodology that Terraform uses to set up and manage infrastructure. It is immediately connected to this idea, which leads straight to the concept.

Following that, we were familiar with the use of Terraform to manage a variety of networking components. The first thing that we concentrated on was virtual private clouds, often known as VPCs. VPCs are an essential component of any cloud architecture. Terraform provides the simplified and consistent creation of virtual private clouds (VPCs), as well as their modification and administration. After getting a handle on virtual private clouds (VPCs), we switched our focus to the management of subnets and routing. We went over how to set up routing tables and rules to manage network traffic, as well as how to construct subnets inside of a virtual private cloud (VPC). Additionally, we investigated the DNS administration features of Terraform and discussed how it may assist in the maintenance of DNS records and zones.

In the final part of our discussion, we dug into more difficult topics such as the management of load balancers and the automated scaling of resources. We studied how to auto-scale resources depending on a set of parameters, and we talked about how to use Terraform to design and operate load balancers. When it comes to working with Terraform and network setups, we also brought attention to the significance of troubleshooting and discussed common problems along with the remedies to those problems. We addressed how to identify and resolve common issues such as missing needed parameters, erroneous references to other resources, overlapping CIDR blocks, and circular dependencies. These issues can be caused by a variety of things, including missing essential parameters.

# CHAPTER 9: ADVANCED TOPICS IN TERRAFORM

# Overview

Welcome to Chapter Nine of our book, 'Terraform for Developers', where we're focusing on equipping you with robust troubleshooting skills for handling common Terraform errors and enhancing performance efficiency. This chapter is strategically designed to tackle key areas of difficulty and confusion, guiding you through the intricacies of Terraform's operations and offering practical strategies for error diagnosis and resolution.

At the beginning of this chapter, we embark on understanding the typology of errors that can arise while working with Terraform. We classify them into syntax, semantic, and runtime errors, each one with its unique challenges and solutions. We will be taking a deep dive into these error types, presenting real-world examples, and offering comprehensive solutions, thereby empowering you to swiftly pinpoint and resolve any issues that may arise in your Terraform code. Following this, we explore how you can boost the performance of your Terraform operations by monitoring and optimizing key performance indicators such as execution time, resource usage, and code efficiency. This section aims to equip you with practical strategies to improve infrastructure build times, enhance code performance, and thereby lower operational costs.

Another crucial aspect we will delve into in this chapter is the import of pre-provisioned infrastructure into Terraform. As we recognize the importance of working with existing resources, we provide specific instruction on importing Azure resources, demonstrating how you can easily bring already provisioned infrastructure under Terraform's management. In the latter part of the chapter, we dedicate extensive attention to the practice of testing in Terraform. We explore four main types of testing: unit testing, integration testing, validation testing, and compliance testing. Through a series of illustrative examples, we aim to help you understand the unique value each type of testing provides and how it contributes to the overall reliability of your infrastructure.

We conclude this chapter with a discussion on integrating Terraform into continuous integration and continuous delivery (CI/CD) pipelines, looking specifically at how you can leverage version control systems and tools like GitHub Actions to automate the build, test, and deployment of your infrastructure changes. Through this, we hope to enhance your understanding of how to bring consistency, reduce risk, and inspire confidence in your Terraform-powered infrastructure deployments.

# Categories of Errors

As you continue working with Terraform, it's critical to understand that you will inevitably encounter errors. These errors can broadly be categorized into syntax errors, semantic errors, and runtime errors.

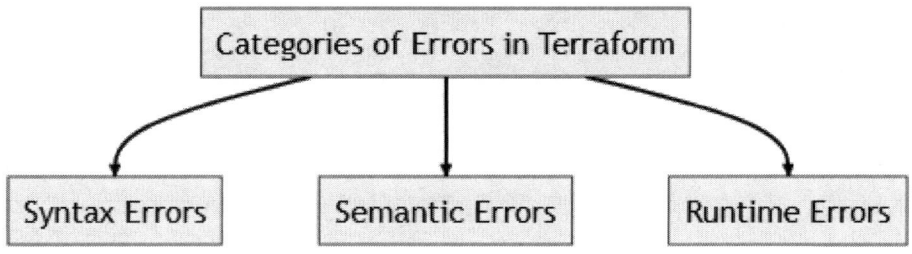

Fig 9.1 Error Types in Terraform

## Syntax Errors

These are the most basic types of errors, which occur when you make a typo or forget to include necessary syntax elements in the Terraform configuration. Terraform has a specific syntax for defining resources, variables, outputs, etc., and any deviation from this syntax will result in a syntax error. For example, forgetting to close a block with '}' or incorrectly using '=' instead of ':' can lead to a syntax error.

```
resource "azurerm_virtual_network" "vnet" { // Missing '{' here will cause a
syntax error
  name            = "acctvn"
  address_space   = ["10.0.0.0/16"]
  location        = azurerm_resource_group.example.location
  resource_group_name = azurerm_resource_group.example.name
```

## Semantic Errors

These errors occur when the Terraform configuration is syntactically correct but doesn't make sense to the Terraform interpreter. These can often be harder to detect as the syntax appears to be correct. For example, referring to an undefined variable, referencing an output from a module that doesn't exist, or providing an incorrect data type to a resource argument can all result in semantic errors.

```
resource "azurerm_virtual_network" "vnet" {
  name            = "acctvn"
  address_space   = ["10.0.0.0/16"]
  location        = azurerm_resource_group.example.location
```

```
  resource_group_name = azurerm_resource_group.example.name
  depends_on          = ["azurerm_resource_group.non_existing_resource"] //
Semantic error: non-existing resource
}
```

## Runtime Errors

These errors occur when the Terraform configuration is both syntactically and semantically correct, but an error occurs when interacting with the remote system (in this case, the Azure provider). Examples include network connectivity issues, API rate limits being exceeded, or incorrect access permissions on the Azure account.

```
resource "azurerm_virtual_network" "vnet" {
  name            = "acctvn"
  address_space   = ["10.0.0.0/16"]
  location        = azurerm_resource_group.example.location
  resource_group_name = azurerm_resource_group.example.name
} // This configuration will cause a runtime error if the Azure account doesn't
have permission to create a VNet
```

Another set of errors can be related to Terraform state. These could occur when there's a mismatch between the actual infrastructure and the Terraform state, also known as 'drift'. Inconsistent state file access between team members might also lead to state conflicts.

# Troubleshooting Syntax Errors

Syntax errors in Terraform can be a bit challenging to understand initially, but as you work with Terraform more, you will become accustomed to its syntax and the types of syntax errors that can occur. Let us proceed to look at a practical example where a syntax error might occur, and how to resolve it.

Suppose you're defining a Virtual Network in Azure using the azurerm_virtual_network resource, but you accidentally omit a bracket. The Terraform configuration might look something like this:

```
resource "azurerm_virtual_network" "example"
  name            = "example-network"
```

```
  location          = azurerm_resource_group.example.location
  resource_group_name = azurerm_resource_group.example.name
  address_space     = ["10.0.0.0/16"]
}
```

When you run terraform apply, Terraform will return an error because it's expecting a bracket before the resource attributes. The error message might look something like this:

Error: Missing '{'

on main.tf line 2:
  2: resource "azurerm_virtual_network" "example"

A block definition must have block content delimited by "{", and "}",
In this case, the error message is helpful because it tells you exactly what's wrong: it's missing a '{'. We can then add the '{' after the resource name, like so:

```
resource "azurerm_virtual_network" "example" {
  name              = "example-network"
  location          = azurerm_resource_group.example.location
  resource_group_name = azurerm_resource_group.example.name
  address_space     = ["10.0.0.0/16"]
}
```

Another common syntax error might occur if you incorrectly use '=' instead of ':' to define an argument. If you did that in the example above, the configuration might look something like this:

```
resource "azurerm_virtual_network" "example" {
  name              = "example-network"
  location          = azurerm_resource_group.example.location
  resource_group_name = azurerm_resource_group.example.name
  address_space     = ["10.0.0.0/16"]
}
```

When you run terraform apply, Terraform will return an error because it's expecting a ':' after 'resource'. The error message might look something like this:

Error: Invalid argument name

on main.tf line 3, in resource "azurerm_virtual_network" "example":
 3:   name            = "example-network"

Argument names must not be quoted.

In this case, you can correct the error by replacing the '=' with a ':', like so:

```
resource "azurerm_virtual_network" "example" {
  name              = "example-network"
  location          = azurerm_resource_group.example.location
  resource_group_name = azurerm_resource_group.example.name
  address_space     = ["10.0.0.0/16"]
}
```

One of the best ways to avoid syntax errors is to use a code editor that supports Terraform syntax highlighting and auto-completion, such as VS Code with the HashiCorp Terraform extension. This can help catch syntax errors before you even run terraform apply.

# Troubleshooting Semantic Errors

Semantic errors in Terraform happen when the code is syntactically correct, but the logic of the code is incorrect. These are more challenging to debug because the code seems fine at a glance. This type of error often happens when you're using a property or attribute incorrectly, referencing an invalid resource, or misconfiguration of a resource.

Let us consider a scenario where you're setting up a virtual network in Azure. If you mistakenly attempt to use an invalid subnet range that is not within the address space of the virtual network, you will encounter a semantic error.

Consider the following Terraform configuration:

```
resource "azurerm_virtual_network" "example" {
  name             = "example-network"
  location         = azurerm_resource_group.example.location
  resource_group_name = azurerm_resource_group.example.name
  address_space    = ["10.0.0.0/16"]
}


resource "azurerm_subnet" "example" {
  name             = "example-subnet"
  resource_group_name  = azurerm_resource_group.example.name
  virtual_network_name = azurerm_virtual_network.example.name
  address_prefixes     = ["10.1.0.0/24"]
}
```

In this configuration, the subnet's address prefix is not within the virtual network's address space. Running terraform apply would result in a semantic error like the following:

Error: Subnet's prefix is not within the parent network's address prefix.

The error message is suggesting that there is an inconsistency between the parent network and the subnet's prefix. The solution would be to change the subnet's address prefix to something within the virtual network's address space, like so:

```
resource "azurerm_subnet" "example" {
  name             = "example-subnet"
  resource_group_name  = azurerm_resource_group.example.name
  virtual_network_name = azurerm_virtual_network.example.name
  address_prefixes     = ["10.0.1.0/24"]
}
```

Another common semantic error occurs when you reference a non-existing resource. Let us consider a scenario where you're trying to attach a network security group to a subnet, but the network security group doesn't exist.

The Terraform code might look something like this:

```
resource "azurerm_subnet_network_security_group_association" "example" {
  subnet_id               = azurerm_subnet.example.id
  network_security_group_id = azurerm_network_security_group.example.id
}
```

If the azurerm_network_security_group.example resource isn't defined anywhere in the configuration, you'll get an error like this when you run terraform apply:

```
Error: Reference to undeclared resource

A managed resource "azurerm_network_security_group" "example" has not been declared in the root module.
```

The solution here is to either declare the azurerm_network_security_group.example resource in the configuration or to correct the resource reference in the azurerm_subnet_network_security_group_association resource.

Remember, while syntax errors involve incorrect code structure, semantic errors involve incorrect code logic. Semantic errors require a deeper understanding of how Terraform and its providers work, which comes with practice and experience

# Troubleshooting Runtime Errors

Runtime errors occur when the Terraform configuration is syntactically correct and semantically valid, but something goes wrong during execution. This can happen due to issues such as network problems, API rate limits, insufficient permissions, or unavailable resources. Let us proceed to walk through some examples.

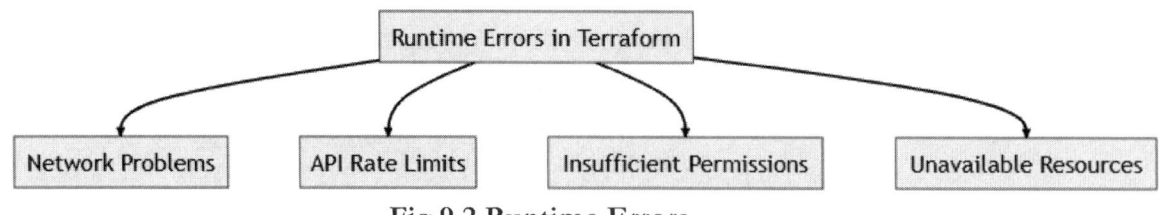

**Fig 9.2 Runtime Errors**

# API Rate Limiting

Terraform interacts with the cloud providers through their APIs. If you are creating, updating, or deleting a large number of resources within a short period of time, you may hit the API rate limit. For example, in Azure, you might see an error like this:

Error: Error creating Network Security Rule:
network.SecurityRulesClient#CreateOrUpdate: Failure responding to request:
StatusCode=429 -- Original Error: autorest/azure: Service returned an error.
Status=429 Code="TooManyRequests" Message="The server rejected the request because too many requests have been received for this subscription."

This indicates that too many requests were sent within a specific timeframe. The resolution here would typically be to either rate limit the requests or to spread the resource deployment over time.

# Insufficient Permissions

If the Terraform service account or user doesn't have the necessary permissions to create, update, or delete a resource, you will encounter a runtime error. For example, you might encounter an error like this when creating a virtual network in Azure:

Error: Error Creating/Updating Virtual Network "myVNet" (Resource Group "myResourceGroup"): network.VirtualNetworksClient#CreateOrUpdate: Failure sending request: StatusCode=403 -- Original Error: Code="AuthorizationFailed" Message="The client '12345678-9abc-def0-1234-56789abcdef0' with object id '12345678-9abc-def0-1234-56789abcdef0' does not have authorization to perform action 'Microsoft.Network/virtualNetworks/write' over scope '/subscriptions/12345678-9abc-def0-1234-56789abcdef0/resourceGroups/myResourceGroup/providers/Microsoft.Network/virtualNetworks/myVNet' or the scope is invalid. If access was recently granted, please refresh the credentials."

This error is saying that the user does not have sufficient permissions to create or modify a virtual network. The solution is to either grant the necessary permissions or to use a different user or service account that has the required permissions.

## Unavailable Resources

Sometimes, you might try to create a resource that is not available in the selected region. For instance, certain VM sizes may not be available in all Azure regions. If you try to create such a resource, you'll encounter an error message like this:

```
Error: Error creating Linux Virtual Machine "example" (Resource Group
"example"): compute.VirtualMachinesClient#CreateOrUpdate: Failure sending
request: StatusCode=400 -- Original Error: Code="InvalidParameter"
Message="The requested size for resource '/subscriptions/12345678-9abc-def0-
1234-
56789abcdef0/resourceGroups/example/providers/Microsoft.Compute/virtualM
achines/example' is currently not available in location 'eastus' zones " for
subscription '12345678-9abc-def0-1234-56789abcdef0'. Please try another size or
deploy to a different location or zones. See https://aka.ms/azureskunotavailable
for details."
```

In such cases, the solution would be to either select a different VM size that's available in the region or to choose a different region where the desired VM size is available.

By understanding the nature of these runtime errors, you can strategize their mitigation more effectively. Carefully read the error messages you receive, as they often include clues about the problem's root cause and potential solutions.

# Terraform Performance Indicators (KPI)

Understanding the Key Performance Indicators (KPIs) for Terraform is crucial to ensuring the infrastructure's smooth operation and optimizing the workflows. In the context of Terraform, performance can be assessed using several KPIs, including execution speed, resource utilization, error rates, and maintainability. Let us proceed to delve into each one.

## Execution Speed

This is one of the most direct measures of Terraform performance. It's measured by the time taken to execute the 'terraform apply' command, including the time taken to plan, create, update, or destroy resources. It depends on several factors including the number and type of resources being managed, the cloud provider's API response times, and the network latency. This metric helps you understand if the Terraform scripts are optimized and if the underlying resources are performing as expected.

To optimize execution speed, focus on reducing the complexity of the Terraform configurations. Use parallel resource creation where possible and asynchronous provisioning techniques. Below is the example of asynchronous resource creation using the count parameter:

```
resource "aws_instance" "app" {
  count = 10
  ami         = "ami-0c94855ba95c574c8"
  instance_type = "t2.micro"
}
```

The above code would create 10 instances in parallel, reducing the time taken by the terraform apply command.

# Resource Utilization

This refers to the extent of cloud resources usage by the Terraform configurations. Understanding this KPI can help optimize costs and usage, particularly in cloud environments where resources are paid for. We can monitor metrics such as CPU utilization, memory usage, network bandwidth usage, and disk I/O operations. Higher than usual resource utilization might indicate inefficient Terraform code, requiring refactoring or optimization. Tools like AWS CloudWatch, Google Cloud's Stackdriver or Azure Monitor can help you track these metrics.

# Error Rates

Measuring error rates includes tracking failed terraform apply runs, syntax or runtime errors, and resource provisioning failures. A low error rate indicates that the Terraform code is robust, whereas a high error rate might suggest issues with the code, the cloud provider, or external dependencies. Monitoring error rates over time can provide insights into trends and recurring issues, which can help improve the reliability of the Terraform code.

To reduce error rates, use validation tools like tflint or tfsec to catch errors before applying changes. An example of using tflint could be:

```
$ tflint my_configuration.tf
```

This would validate my_configuration.tf and report any errors, preventing potential failed terraform apply runs.

# Maintainability

This KPI measures how easy it is to manage and adapt the Terraform code. It includes factors such as code readability, use of modules, adherence to DRY (Don't Repeat Yourself) principle, and the level of documentation. Well-structured, modularized, and well-documented code is easier to maintain and less prone to errors, thus improving overall performance. Tools like tflint or tfsec can help ensure the code adheres to best practices, improving its maintainability.

For instance, here is how to use a module:

```
module "vpc" {
  source = "terraform-aws-modules/vpc/aws"
  version = "2.77.0"
  name = "my-vpc"
  cidr = "10.0.0.0/16"
}
```

This creates a VPC using the module terraform-aws-modules/vpc/aws, enhancing code reusability and readability.

# Deployment Frequency

This KPI measures the number of times the team applies changes to the infrastructure using Terraform. A higher deployment frequency often indicates a mature DevOps culture and an efficient use of Terraform, as it suggests that the team is able to make small, incremental changes to the infrastructure safely and quickly.

# Change Lead Time

This KPI measures the amount of time it takes from when a change is committed, until that change is successfully applied in the environment. This will depend on factors such as the complexity of the Terraform code, the number of environments to which changes need to be deployed, and the efficiency of the deployment pipelines.

Carefully evaluating key performance indicators like plan/apply duration, resource usage, and code maintainability provides critical insight into the real-world performance of Terraform. Analyzing these metrics enables practitioners to pinpoint opportunities for optimization, address reliability risks, and ensure infrastructure management is efficient, cost-effective, and aligned with best practices. Considering KPIs takes an analytical approach that promotes continuous improvement - allowing teams to not just operationalize Terraform but master it across scale, security, costs, and collaboration.

# Import Existing Infrastructure

Importing existing infrastructure into Terraform allows you to manage resources that were not initially created by Terraform, a common use case when integrating Terraform into an existing infrastructure setup.

The general process of importing resources into Terraform involves:
- Writing a resource configuration block in the Terraform configuration that corresponds to the resource you want to import.
- Running terraform import <RESOURCE.NAME> <RESOURCE_ID>, where RESOURCE.NAME is the address of the resource configuration block in the Terraform configuration and RESOURCE_ID is the ID of the existing resource.

Let us proceed to use Azure Resource Group as an example. Suppose you have an existing Resource Group in Azure named my-resource-group.

First, define the resource block in the Terraform configuration file, main.tf:

```
provider "azurerm" {
  features {}
}


resource "azurerm_resource_group" "rg" {
  name = "my-resource-group"
  location = "West US"
}
```

In this case, the resource address is azurerm_resource_group.rg.

To get the ID of the existing Resource Group, you can use Azure CLI command az group show --name my-resource-group --query id --output tsv, which will return something like

/subscriptions/00000000-0000-0000-0000-000000000000/resourceGroups/my-resource-group.

To import the resource, run terraform import azurerm_resource_group.rg /subscriptions/00000000-0000-0000-0000-000000000000/resourceGroups/my-resource-group.

Terraform will fetch the current state of the resource from Azure and compare it to the configuration you wrote. If everything matches, Terraform will consider the resource under its management. However, please note that if the existing resource configuration in Azure differs from what you've declared in the main.tf file, the terraform import command will fail. Therefore, it's crucial that the Terraform configuration accurately reflects the current state of the resource in Azure.

Moreover, the terraform import command does not generate configuration. We must create a configuration for each resource that matches the current state, then use terraform import to attach the existing resource to that configuration. If you're dealing with a large number of resources, there are third-party tools like terraformer that can help generate these configurations, but they are outside the scope of core Terraform functionality.

# Terraform Testing Overview

Testing is a crucial aspect of any development process, and in the context of Terraform, it helps to verify the correctness of the Terraform configurations, ensure the integrity of the infrastructure, and prevent inadvertent destructive changes. In Terraform, testing can be divided into several categories: Unit Testing, Integration Testing, Validation Testing, and Compliance Testing.

## Unit Testing

This is the lowest level of testing where individual components (like modules in Terraform) are tested in isolation. In Terraform, a 'unit' might be a single resource or a module. Unit testing in Terraform involves creating configurations with varying inputs and asserting that the plan's outputs are as expected. This can be done using the terraform plan command, which shows what actions Terraform will take to reach the desired state defined in the configuration without actually applying those changes. Some third-party tools such as terratest can facilitate unit testing in Terraform.

For example, suppose you have a module for creating an Azure virtual machine. A unit test might involve creating a configuration that calls this module with specific inputs and then asserting that the plan includes creating a VM with those specifications.

# Integration Testing

While unit tests verify individual components, integration tests ensure that the components work correctly when combined. In Terraform, this might involve ensuring that the resources created by one module interact correctly with resources managed by another module. Like unit testing, third-party tools such as terratest are often used to facilitate integration testing.

For instance, if you have a module that creates a VNet and another that creates a VM, an integration test might involve creating a configuration that uses both modules to ensure that the VM is correctly associated with the VNet.

# Validation Testing

Validation tests ensure that the infrastructure is in the desired state after the Terraform configurations have been applied. This can be done manually by checking the state of the resources through the provider's console or CLI, or it can be automated using tools like terraform-compliance or even by scripting calls to the provider's API.

For example, after using Terraform to create an Azure virtual machine, a validation test might involve using the Azure CLI to check that the VM is in the expected state and has the correct settings.

# Compliance Testing

Compliance tests check that the configurations adhere to best practices and organizational policies. Tools such as tfsec or checkov can scan the Terraform code for common security issues or misconfigurations and can be integrated into a CI/CD pipeline to catch potential issues before the code is applied.

As an example, if the organization has a policy that all Azure Storage Accounts must be encrypted, a compliance test might involve using tfsec to scan the configurations and fail the test if it finds an unencrypted storage account.

It's important to note that testing in Terraform doesn't have a one-size-fits-all solution. The scope and nature of the tests will depend on factors like the complexity of the infrastructure, the needs of the organization, and the compliance requirements. Therefore, it's crucial to develop a thorough testing strategy that covers the various stages of the infrastructure lifecycle.

# Executing Unit Testing

For executing unit tests in Terraform, we often use a third-party tool called Terratest. Terratest is a Go library that provides patterns and helper functions for testing infrastructure, with first-class support for Terraform. Please note that you should have a basic understanding of Go language syntax for writing and understanding Terratest tests.

Before we dive into the example, let us set up Terratest in the project. We need to have Go installed in the machine. Create a new directory in the project called "test", navigate into it and run go mod init, this will create a new go.mod file. In the same directory, create a new go file (for instance, vm_test.go) and add the following content:

```go
package test

import (
    "testing"

    "github.com/gruntwork-io/terratest/modules/terraform"
    "github.com/stretchr/testify/assert"
)

func TestTerraformAzureExample(t *testing.T) {
    // Construct the terraform options with default retryable errors to handle the most common retryable errors in
    // terraform testing.
    terraformOptions := &terraform.Options{
        // The path to where the Terraform code is located
        TerraformDir: "../",
    }

    // Run `terraform init` and `terraform apply` and fail the test if there are any errors
    terraform.InitAndApply(t, terraformOptions)

    // Run `terraform output` to get the value of an output variable
```

```
    vmName := terraform.Output(t, terraformOptions, "vm_name")

    // Verify we're getting back the outputs we expect
    assert.Equal(t, "test_vm", vmName)
}
```

In the above given unit testing sample program, we're testing a Terraform configuration that creates an Azure virtual machine. This test will run terraform init and terraform apply on the configuration, and then check that the vm_name output variable's value is "test_vm". If the output is not as expected, the test will fail.

The Terraform configuration (main.tf) might look something like this:

```
resource "azurerm_virtual_machine" "example" {
  name            = "test_vm"
  // other necessary attributes here...
}

output "vm_name" {
  value = azurerm_virtual_machine.example.name
}
```

The vm_test.go file should be placed in a separate test directory, not in the same directory as the Terraform files. To run the test, you can use the go test command from the test directory:

```
go test -v
```

This command will take a few minutes to run, as it is actually creating resources in Azure. It will display the test results in the console when it's done.

Briefly put, a unit test in Terraform employing Terratest is a method of confirming the outcome of a configuration by spawning actual resources. This provides a high degree of confidence in the behavior of the Terraform modules, but it can cause the process to take longer and cost more money. This is because resources are produced and destroyed in the cloud provider. As a result, it is typically utilized in conjunction with several other types of testing, such as integration testing and static code analysis.

# Implementing Integration Testing

Continuing from where we left off with Terratest, let us dive into how we can use it to perform integration testing on our Terraform code. An integration test in the context of Terraform is testing multiple modules together as a cohesive unit to verify that they interact with each other correctly.

Consider an example where we have two Terraform modules: one that creates a Virtual Network in Azure and another that creates a Virtual Machine. The Virtual Machine is supposed to be created within the Virtual Network. We want to test that these modules correctly integrate with each other.

Our project structure might look something like this:

```
.
├── main.tf
├── modules
│   ├── virtual_machine
│   │   └── main.tf
│   └── virtual_network
│       └── main.tf
└── test
    └── integration_test.go
```

In our main.tf, we have something like this:

```
module "virtual_network" {
  source = "./modules/virtual_network"
  // other necessary variables here...
}

module "virtual_machine" {
  source = "./modules/virtual_machine"
  network_id = module.virtual_network.network_id
```

```
// other necessary variables here...
}

output "vm_id" {
  value = module.virtual_machine.vm_id
}

output "network_id" {
  value = module.virtual_network.network_id
}
```

Our integration_test.go might look like this:

```
package test

import (
    "testing"

    "github.com/gruntwork-io/terratest/modules/terraform"
    "github.com/stretchr/testify/assert"
)

func TestTerraformIntegrationExample(t *testing.T) {
    // Construct the terraform options with default retryable errors to handle the most common retryable errors in
    // terraform testing.
    terraformOptions := &terraform.Options{
        // The path to where the Terraform code is located
        TerraformDir: "../",
    }

    // Run `terraform init` and `terraform apply` and fail the test if there are any errors
```

```
    terraform.InitAndApply(t, terraformOptions)

    // Run `terraform output` to get the value of output variables
    vmID := terraform.Output(t, terraformOptions, "vm_id")
    networkID := terraform.Output(t, terraformOptions, "network_id")

    // Perform some assertions to check whether the resources are properly
integrated
    // The details of these assertions will depend on the use-case. It could be a
simple as checking if IDs are non-empty,
    // or it might involve more complicated checks involving querying the Azure
API and verifying resource attributes.
    assert.NotEmpty(t, vmID)
    assert.NotEmpty(t, networkID)
    // more assertions here as needed...
}
```

As with our unit test example, we run this test using go test -v. This will apply the configuration and perform the assertions, and then automatically run terraform destroy at the end to clean up the resources.

To reiterate, an integration test verifies that multiple Terraform modules work together as expected. This can provide a high degree of confidence in the infrastructure's behavior, but it can also take a while to run and cost money, as resources are created and destroyed in the cloud provider. It's a crucial part of a comprehensive testing strategy for the Terraform code.

# Running Validation Testing

Terraform validation testing focuses on validating the correctness of the provisioned infrastructure itself, not just the code. It goes beyond syntax checks or integration testing between components. Validation testing asserts whether the deployed infrastructure matches the intended functionality, business goals, and requirements. This testing discipline verifies the end-to-end behavior of the infrastructure from the operator's perspective, ensuring the production environment is functioning as designed. Whereas other test types narrow in on code, validation testing takes a broad view validating the total system against real-world needs.

We can use Terratest for validation testing as well, by executing HTTP checks against the deployed resources or making API calls to the cloud provider to check the state of the resources.

Let us continue from our previous example. We have our VM created inside a VNet in Azure. Let us imagine that this VM is running a web application that we can reach by using its public IP address. Our goal now is to verify that this web application responds to HTTP requests correctly.

The validation_test.go could look something like this:

```
package test

import (
    "testing"
    "time"

    "github.com/gruntwork-io/terratest/modules/terraform"
    "github.com/gruntwork-io/terratest/modules/http-helper"
)

func TestTerraformValidationExample(t *testing.T) {
    terraformOptions := &terraform.Options{
        TerraformDir: "../",
    }

    // Deploy the infrastructure
    terraform.InitAndApply(t, terraformOptions)

    // Obtain the public IP of the VM
    vmIP := terraform.Output(t, terraformOptions, "vm_ip")

    // Define the URL of the web application
```

```
    url := "http://" + vmIP + ":8080"

    // Define the expected HTTP status code and body
    expectedStatus := 200
    expectedBody := "Hello, World!"

    // Set a timeout for the HTTP check
    maxRetries := 30
    timeBetweenRetries := 5 * time.Second

    // Check the HTTP response
    http_helper.HttpGetWithRetry(t, url, expectedStatus, expectedBody,
maxRetries, timeBetweenRetries)
}
```

In the above given validation testing sample program, we are using Terratest's http_helper package. The HttpGetWithRetry function sends HTTP GET requests to the specified URL and checks that the response matches the expected status code and body. The test will fail if it doesn't match after the specified number of retries.

It's worth noting that validation testing is close to end-to-end testing in the infrastructure testing domain. This type of testing can be complex and time-consuming, but it's essential for validating that the Terraform code behaves as expected when deployed to the actual infrastructure environment.

As always, the sophistication of the tests depends on the particular requirements and the complexity of the infrastructure. This above sample program only scratches the surface of what you can do with validation testing in Terraform.

# Testing Compliance

Compliance testing for infrastructure as code involves validating adherence to defined standards and policies. This could include organizational best practices, security guidelines, regulatory obligations, or other governance requirements. The goal is to guarantee infrastructure deployments comply with all applicable norms. A powerful tool for implementing compliance testing in Terraform is Open Policy Agent (OPA). It uses the Rego policy language to evaluate Terraform plans against custom-defined guardrails and constraints.

For example, Rego policies could check that all Azure resources have mandatory tags, storage is encrypted, or sensitive data handling follows regulations. Any non-compliant resources would be blocked from applying. In this way, OPA and Rego allow baking organizational and regulatory compliance directly into the Terraform deployments. Compliance testing shifts security and governance left, preventing unapproved infrastructure changes before provisioning.

Let us create a compliance test to ensure that all our Azure resources are correctly tagged with an "environment" tag.

First, we'll write our policy in Rego:

```
package main

# Rule for missing tags
missing_tags[resource_type] {
    some resource_type
    input.resource_changes[_].type = resource_type
    input.resource_changes[_].change.after.tags == null
}

# Rule for missing environment tag
missing_env_tag[resource_type] {
    some resource_type
    input.resource_changes[_].type = resource_type
    tags := input.resource_changes[_].change.after.tags
    not tags["environment"]
}
```

This policy has two rules. The first one, missing_tags, checks if there are any resources without a tags attribute. The second one, missing_env_tag, checks if there are any resources with tags, but missing the environment tag.

To use this policy, we need to generate a JSON representation of our Terraform plan:

```
terraform plan -out=tfplan.binary
terraform show -json tfplan.binary > tfplan.json
```

This will produce a file named tfplan.json that we can feed into OPA:

```
opa eval --format pretty --data policy.rego --input tfplan.json "data"
```

This command does an analysis of the policy in light of our Terraform plan. In the event that any of the policy's rules are satisfied, OPA will produce a list of the resource categories that are in violation of the regulations. Making use of automated compliance tests like these helps to ensure that incorrect configurations do not make it into production. It is a potent instrument for assuring compliance with the organizational or project-specific standards because, with OPA and Rego, you can specify rules for nearly any part of the Terraform code. This makes it possible to use the instrument to manage compliance issues.

# Working with CI/CD

Integrating Terraform into a Continuous Integration/Continuous Delivery (CI/CD) pipeline is a crucial aspect of achieving complete automation in the software delivery process. The primary objective of CI/CD is to create a system that is not only automated but also reliable and repeatable for delivering software. When it comes to Infrastructure as Code (IaC) tools like Terraform, this translates into the delivery and updating of cloud resources in an automated and consistent manner.

In the context of a CI/CD pipeline, Terraform plays a pivotal role in managing and provisioning the infrastructure needed by your application. It allows you to script your infrastructure setup and changes, which can then be version controlled and tested just like your application code. This brings a lot of benefits, such as the ability to review infrastructure changes, roll back to a previous state if something goes wrong, and create consistent environments for development, testing, and production.

A basic pipeline may consist of:
- Developer commits Terraform config changes to a Git repo
- Continuous integration server detects change and kicks off workflow
- Terraform syntax validated, security scans run
- Terraform plan generated to preview changes
- Apply executed in a test environment matched to production
- Automated tests validate functionality and correctness
- Upon success, changes are approved and promoted to production

- Production credentials used to orchestrate final deployment

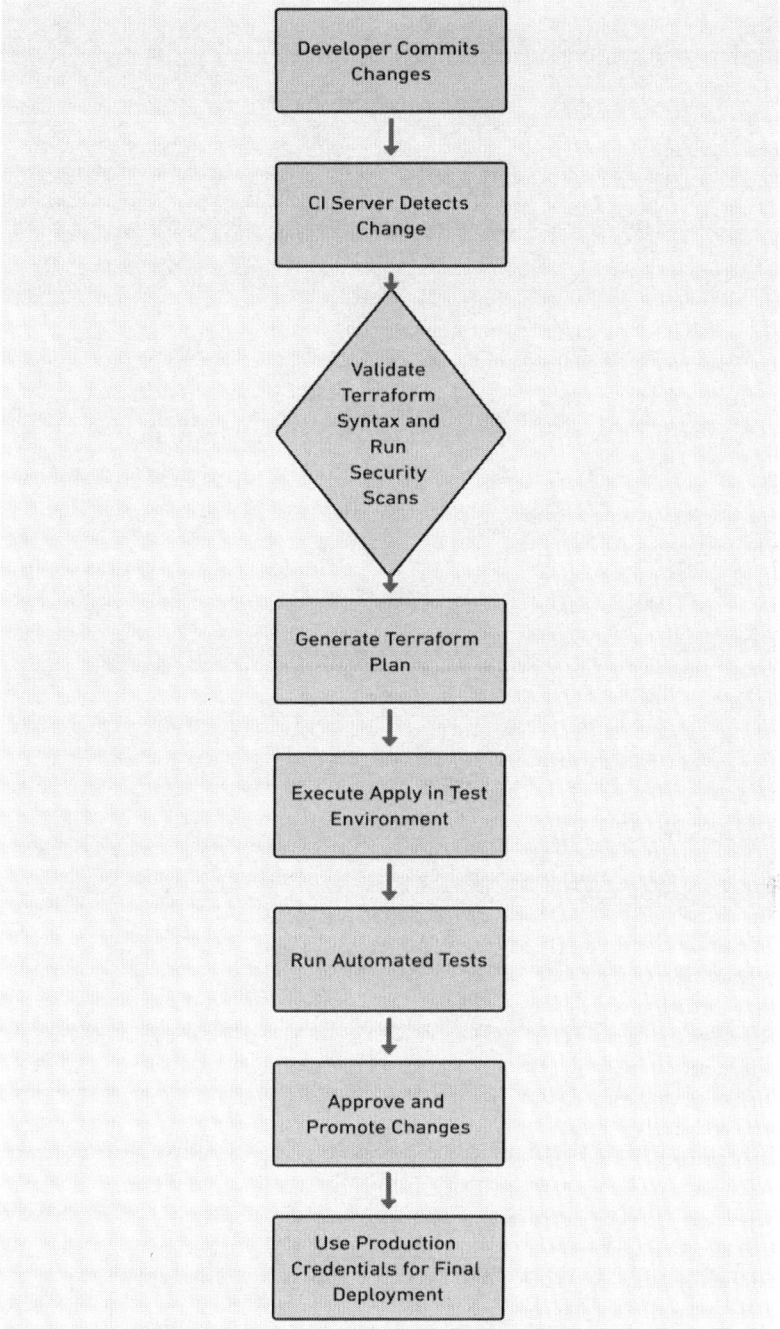

**Fig 9.3 Terraform CI/CD pipeline**

This automated workflow ensures infrastructure changes can be frequently delivered at high velocity while still preserving safety, stability, and compliance.

Let us consider a simple pipeline with following steps:

## Source Control

This is where the Terraform code resides. It's best practice to use a version control system like Git, which allows you to track changes, collaborate with others, and revert to previous states if needed.

## Continuous Integration

In this stage, you'll validate the Terraform code. This typically involves syntax checks and unit tests, and in Terraform, this can be done with commands like terraform validate and terraform plan. We might also integrate a linter or style checker, like tflint or tfsec, to enforce coding standards and security best practices.

```
terraform init
terraform validate
tflint
tfsec
```

## Continuous Delivery

After the code has been validated and the tests have passed, you're ready to deliver the infrastructure. In Terraform, this means running terraform apply. In a production environment, you'll likely need to run this in an automated manner, which will require setting up the proper permissions and environment variables.

```
terraform apply -auto-approve
```

It's important to remember that the -auto-approve flag should be used cautiously, since it automatically applies changes without manual intervention.

## Infrastructure Monitoring and Observability

After the resources have been delivered, you'll want to monitor them to ensure they're behaving as expected. We might use a tool like Prometheus, Grafana, or Azure Monitor, depending on the cloud provider and needs.

For the CI/CD pipeline, you can use a variety of tools, such as Jenkins, GitLab CI/CD, GitHub Actions, or Azure DevOps. For example, with GitHub Actions, you can set up workflows that trigger on certain events (like a push to the main branch) and run jobs (like terraform apply) in response.

## Sample Program of GitHub Actions Workflow

Following is a simple example of a GitHub Actions workflow for Terraform:

```
name: 'Terraform CI'

on:
  push:
    branches:
    - main

jobs:
  terraform:
    name: 'Terraform'
    runs-on: ubuntu-latest

    steps:
    - name: Checkout
      uses: actions/checkout@v2

    - name: Setup Terraform
      uses: hashicorp/setup-terraform@v1
      with:
        terraform_version: 1.0.0

    - name: Terraform Init
      run: terraform init
```

```
- name: Terraform Validate
  run: terraform validate

- name: Terraform Plan
  run: terraform plan

- name: Terraform Apply
  run: terraform apply -auto-approve
```

This workflow checks out the code, sets up Terraform, initializes the Terraform configuration, validates the configuration, and then applies the changes. Of course, in a real-world setting, you'd want to customize this to suit the needs and follow best practices around handling sensitive data and approvals.

Integrating Terraform with CI/CD not only automates the delivery of the infrastructure but also ensures consistency and reliability in the deployments.

# Summary

Chapter nine focused on building troubleshooting skills for common Terraform errors and performance issues. We began by classifying errors into three types - syntax, semantic, and runtime. Syntax errors relate to improperly formatted code, semantic errors arise from flawed program logic, and runtime errors occur during execution. Recognizing the source of each error is critical for quick diagnosis and resolution. Practical debugging strategies were presented to tackle errors head on.

We then explored key Terraform performance indicators including execution time, resource usage, and code efficiency. Monitoring and optimizing these metrics can significantly improve infrastructure build times and lower costs. Use cases were provided to demonstrate performance tuning in action. The ability to import existing resources into Terraform was also covered, enabling pre-provisioned infrastructure to come under Terraform's management. We specifically looked at importing Azure resources to see this capability firsthand.

The chapter concluded with a deep look at testing Terraform code. Unit testing validates individual components while integration testing verifies the connections between components. Validation testing checks the correctness of the infrastructure itself and compliance testing audits against regulatory standards. Each testing approach was exemplified through illustrative examples. Testing improves infrastructure reliability by catching issues early.

Finally, we examined integrating Terraform into continuous integration and continuous delivery (CI/CD) pipelines. Storing Terraform configuration in version control enables collaboration and sets the foundation for automation. CI/CD tooling like GitHub Actions can then build, test, and deploy infrastructure changes automatically. The result is enhanced consistency, reduced risk, and greater confidence in infrastructure deployments powered by Terraform.

# CHAPTER 10:
# ADMINISTERING
# TERRAFORM AS EXPERT

# Overview

This chapter promises to elucidate some of the more intricate aspects of this powerful tool, focusing primarily on the creation of modular code components, secrets management, Kubernetes deployment in Azure, and management of container images and metadata. As we prepare to begin our final investigation into Terraform's advanced capabilities, this chapter promises to elucidate some of the more intricate aspects of Terraform. We are able to considerably improve the speed and stability of our deployments thanks to the modular code components that are provided by Terraform. These components provide us the flexibility to package infrastructure parts, which makes it simple for several teams to easily share these packages. By moving away from monolithic code architectures, which can be difficult to manage, the use of modules promotes an atmosphere that is conducive to cooperation and increases overall productivity. It is impossible to emphasize the significance of security, which is why we go further into the utilization of HashiCorp Vault, a potent application that manages secrets and sensitive data in a secure manner and has been covered previously. Vault does away with the need for using static passwords and keys by enabling the development of ephemeral credentials that can be generated on the fly. The increased automation and level of abstraction bring about major improvements for both the operations and the security of the system.

After that, we get into the nitty-gritty of actually installing a Kubernetes cluster inside of Azure, which is the next step. We will discuss the needs, such as resource groups, virtual networks, and subnets, as we walk you through the intricate process of constructing an Azure Kubernetes Service (AKS) cluster and guide you through its complexities. Even though the installation of a Kubernetes cluster could appear to be a simple process, production-grade deployments require careful attention to the most minute details of its networking and configuration in order to get optimal results. At long last, we will investigate Terraform's capacity to manage container images as well as metadata. We will illustrate how Terraform can create and deploy Kubernetes clusters and apps in addition to managing compute, network, and storage resources as a way to highlight its adaptability.

This chapter demonstrates how Terraform may be used in a variety of different areas of today's technology infrastructure, bringing together Terraform's wide capabilities in the process. Terraform is an essential tool for managing complexity because it enables you to apply the principles of infrastructure-as-code across a wide range of different technological environments. Terraform's uses include setting base infrastructure, maintaining secrets, and deploying Kubernetes.

# Create Custom Modules

Becoming an expert in creating the own modules and sharing them with the team involves a series of steps, beginning with understanding the need for modules in Terraform and mastering the creation of modular code. As said earlier, modules in Terraform are self-contained packages of Terraform configurations that manage a collection of resources. They provide an easy way to abstract common blocks of code that can be used across multiple projects, enhancing reusability, maintainability, and standardization of the infrastructure code.

First, to create a Terraform module, you must identify the common components that can be abstracted into a module. For instance, suppose you have several Azure virtual machines that need the same network interfaces, disk configurations, and virtual network settings. In that case, you can abstract these into a single module.

Creating a module involves writing a Terraform configuration file that declares the necessary resources, variables, and outputs. For instance, for the Azure virtual machine example, the module might look something like this:

```
variable "vm_name" {}
variable "location" {}

resource "azurerm_virtual_machine" "vm" {
  name     = var.vm_name
  location = var.location

  ...
}
```

This configuration creates a virtual machine in Azure with the specified name and location. The variables allow you to customize the module each time you use it. Once the module is defined, it can be called from any Terraform configuration. The source attribute points to the module location and any required input variables are passed in.

```
module "vm_module" {
  source   = "./modules/vm_module"
  vm_name  = "my_vm"
  location = "West Europe"
```

Next, consider the module structure. A well-organized module can significantly improve code readability and maintainability. Typically, a module should have a main.tf file that contains the main resource definitions, a variables.tf file that declares all the variables the module needs, and an outputs.tf file that defines any values the module exports.

Now that you've decided to share the module with the team, you have a few different alternatives to choose from. We are able to save the modules to a shared file system and utilize the file path in the source attribute if the team is co-located. This is a convenient option. However, using a version control system such as GitHub or a Terraform registry, such as the public Terraform Registry or Terraform Cloud, provides a more scalable approach for distant teams. One example of such a registry is Terraform Cloud. We are able to store the modules in a directory structure within a GitHub repository that is appropriate for the organization, if you so choose. After that, you can use the source property in the Terraform configuration to direct the configuration to this repository. We may also tag a specific version of the module in GitHub, which will allow the team to utilize a reliable version of the module while you continue to develop it. This option is available to you if you use the GitHub platform.

Keep in mind that the most important step in becoming a Terraform module creation and sharing expert is to continually improve the modules as you get more expertise and receive feedback from the team. Utilize the modularity of Terraform to your advantage in order to design and share efficient, reusable modules, since this kind of iterative, collaborative approach to the development of infrastructure code is made possible by Terraform's modularity.

# Using Git for Configuration Management

Version control systems play an important role in tracking and monitoring configuration changes, particularly in a Terraform environment. They allow you to track changes made to the code over time, see who made the changes, revert to previous versions if needed, and more importantly, they facilitate a seamless collaboration amongst team members. Git is a widely used distributed version control system and we will discuss its usage in this context.

Terraform configurations are typically stored as code files (with the .tf extension), making them perfectly suited for being managed under version control. This allows developers to keep a historical track of who changed what, when, and why, and it also makes it easier to manage different versions of the infrastructure.

Following is a procedure on how you can use Git to track and monitor the Terraform configuration changes:

# Initialize Git Repository

The initial step towards version control in Terraform begins with initializing a Git Repository. Git is a distributed version control system that allows tracking changes made to the project files. In the terminal, navigate to your directory containing the Terraform configuration files. Here, run the command 'git init'. This command sets up a new Git repository in your current directory, creating a .git folder. This .git folder is a hidden directory that contains all the necessary metadata for the new repository. It's essentially the backbone of your version control environment.

# Commit the Changes

Once you have initialized the Git repository, the subsequent step is to commit changes to it. Making changes to the Terraform configuration could be anything from editing variables, adjusting resource attributes to adding or removing modules. After you've finalized your changes, you'll need to add these changes to the Git repository. Use the command 'git add .' to stage all the changes you've made. Staging changes is like preparing a draft of your changes before committing them to the repository.

After staging, you will commit the changes to the Git repository using the command 'git commit -m "Commit message"'. The '-m' flag lets you attach a descriptive message with the commit, documenting what changes have been made and why. Crafting meaningful commit messages is a crucial practice as it maintains the transparency of project evolution, making it easier for others and your future self to understand the what and why of the changes.

# Push the Changes

The final step, after committing your changes locally, is to make these changes available to your team or the wider community. We can achieve this by pushing your commits to a remote repository such as GitHub or BitBucket. By running 'git push', you send the changes from your local repository to the remote repository. This not only provides a backup of your code but also opens the avenue for collaboration, as others can now access your changes, suggest improvements, or integrate them into their work.

# Accelerate Deployment using Version Control

Now that we have that out of the way, let us talk about how to speed up faster deployment by using version control. Manual processes, which are the conventional way to manage infrastructure deployments, are prone to human mistake and can slow down the deployment process. Automated processes are becoming increasingly popular as an alternative. We can make use of an infrastructure-as-code (IaC) process by putting Terraform configurations in a Git repository. IaC allows you to take advantage of all of the benefits of a software development workflow, including the usage of version control, because the infrastructure setup is defined in code.

When combined with a continuous integration and continuous deployment (CI/CD) technology, such as Jenkins, GitLab CI/CD, or GitHub Actions, deployments can be made to run more quickly while maintaining a higher level of reliability. This strategy may automate the entire process, from deploying infrastructure to committing code and everything in between. When a change is pushed to the Git repository, the CI/CD tool has the ability to automatically pick up the changes, run terraform plan to show what changes will be made, and then run terraform apply to deploy the changes if all goes according to plan.

Let us say you want to use Terraform to manage an AWS EC2 instance, but you realize you need to switch the type of instance you're using. After making the required modification in the.tf file, you use Git to commit the change along with a descriptive statement, and then you push the changes to the repository that is located remotely. The changes are detected and the deployment process is initiated by the CI/CD pipeline in an automated fashion. This method cuts down on the amount of time spent manually intervening, which in turn makes deployments both quicker and less prone to error. In addition to this, it ensures that all modifications are tracked, which makes it simple to determine when and who was responsible for introducing an issue.

The benefits of this approach include:
- Faster deployments by eliminating manual processes
- Safer changes through code reviews and automated testing
- Improved transparency from commit history tracking what, when, who
- Greater productivity by enabling teams to focus on higher value tasks
- Reliability from applying proven software engineering practices

Ultimately, using a version control system with Terraform not only aids in tracking and monitoring configuration changes, but when combined with automation tools, it can greatly accelerate deployment times, while improving transparency and reliability.

# Hashicorp Vault and Dynamic Secrets

HashiCorp Vault is a highly advanced tool for managing secrets and protecting sensitive data. It provides a comprehensive solution for secret management, enabling you to control access to secrets while reducing the risk of data breaches. Vault supports a number of different secret backends, including those for generic secrets, database credentials, SSH credentials, and more.

## Vault's Capabilities

Dynamic Secrets: Vault can generate secrets on-demand for some systems such as AWS or SQL databases. For example, when an application needs to access an Azure SQL database, it asks Vault for credentials, and Vault will create an Azure service principal with the appropriate permissions on the fly.

- Data Encryption: Vault can encrypt and decrypt data without storing it, which simplifies the process of protecting sensitive data that is stored in untrusted or semi-trusted systems.

- Revocable Leases: All secrets in Vault have a lease associated with them. At the end of the lease, Vault automatically revokes the secret. Some secrets have associated actions taken on revocation, for example, dynamic Azure secrets are revoked, the associated service principal is deleted in Azure.

## Generate Dynamic Secrets

To illustrate the process of generating dynamic secrets in Azure with Vault, we'll adhere to a sequence of steps. These include installing and setting up Vault, configuring Vault to connect to Azure, enabling Vault's Azure secrets engine, and finally, creating roles to manage access to Azure resources. The overall process promotes robust security practices, granting on-demand, limited-lifetime access to Azure resources, thereby minimizing the risks associated with static, long-lived credentials.

- Install and start Vault: We first need to have Vault up and running. We can download Vault from the HashiCorp website and follow the instructions to start a Vault dev server.

- Enable Azure secrets engine: After Vault is up and running, the next step is to enable the Azure secrets engine. This can be done using the Vault CLI with the following command: vault secrets enable azure.

- Configure Vault with Azure: After the Azure secrets engine is enabled, you need to configure Vault with the Azure credentials. This is done by writing these credentials to the Azure config in Vault:

```
vault write azure/config \
   subscription_id=SUBSCRIPTION_ID \
   tenant_id=TENANT_ID \
   client_id=CLIENT_ID \
   client_secret=CLIENT_SECRET
```

In the above snippet, replace SUBSCRIPTION_ID, TENANT_ID, CLIENT_ID, and CLIENT_SECRET with the actual Azure credentials.

- Configure a role: Next, you need to configure a role in Vault that maps to a set of permissions in Azure. For instance, to create a role named "my-role" that provides the "Contributor" role scope over a resource group:

```
vault write azure/roles/my-role \
   azure_roles='[
      {
         "role_name": "Contributor",
         "scope": "/subscriptions/SUBSCRIPTION_ID/resourceGroups/my-
resource-group"
      }
   ]'
```

- Generate dynamic secrets: Now you're all set to generate dynamic secrets. Run the following command to generate a new set of credentials:

```
vault read azure/creds/my-role
```

Vault will return a response that includes the client_id and client_secret. These are Azure service principal credentials that have been dynamically generated by Vault. Vault will also automatically handle the lifecycle of this service principal, including its deletion at the end of the lease period.

In this manner, Vault enhances the security of the application environment by providing limited-lifespan, automatically rotated credentials for accessing the Azure resources, thereby minimizing the chances of credentials being compromised. Automating this process could involve integrating Vault with the CI/CD pipeline, or writing a script that fetches dynamic secrets from Vault and feeds them into the application at startup. The overall effect of using dynamic secrets is a greatly reduced attack surface and much stronger security overall. This is because every secret is tightly controlled and can be revoked at will, should there be a risk of a breach.

# Managing Kubernetes Resources

Managing Kubernetes resources using Terraform is an efficient way to ensure consistency and reliability in the Kubernetes infrastructure. Terraform provides the Kubernetes provider that allows you to interact with the resources in a Kubernetes cluster. To start using the Kubernetes provider, you need to specify it in the Terraform configuration and provide the necessary credentials.

Below is an example of how to declare a Kubernetes provider:

```
provider "kubernetes" {
  config_path = "~/.kube/config"
}
```

In this case, we're using config_path to point to the kubeconfig file that provides the necessary connection details. This is the file created by tools like kubectl or minikube.

Let us consider a practical example. Suppose you want to create a Kubernetes namespace using Terraform. Below is how you can define a Kubernetes namespace resource:

```
resource "kubernetes_namespace" "example" {
  metadata {
    name = "example-namespace"
  }
}
```

In the above given sample program, a new Kubernetes namespace called example-namespace will be created.

Next, let us create a deployment in the new namespace:

```
resource "kubernetes_deployment" "example" {
 metadata {
  name = "example-deployment"
  namespace = kubernetes_namespace.example.metadata[0].name
 }

 spec {
  replicas = 3

  selector {
   match_labels = {
     App = "example-app"
   }
  }

  template {
   metadata {
    labels = {
      App = "example-app"
    }
   }

   spec {
    container {
     image = "nginx:1.7.9"
     name  = "example-container"

     port {
      container_port = 80
```

```
      }
     }
    }
   }
  }
 }
}
```

This code creates a deployment in our example-namespace with 3 replicas of an NGINX pod. The kubernetes_namespace.example.metadata[0].name reference ensures the deployment is created in the namespace we created earlier.

We can also manage more complex Kubernetes resources such as services, volumes, and even custom resource definitions (CRDs) with Terraform. The key is to ensure that you've appropriately mapped out the dependencies between the resources and included them in the Terraform configuration. Another important aspect to note is that any changes to the Kubernetes resources can be viewed using the terraform plan command and applied using terraform apply. Terraform allows you to manage the Kubernetes infrastructure in a declarative manner, which simplifies maintaining the desired state of the resources.

# Reference Image Metadata

Referencing image metadata in Terraform, specifically within the context of Microsoft Azure, typically involves interaction with Azure's virtual machine (VM) image resources. Microsoft Azure hosts a gallery of images for VMs, with various OS distributions like Ubuntu, Windows Server, CentOS, etc.

To retrieve an image, you need to know its publisher, offer, SKU, and version. In most cases, Azure's Marketplace maintains these image resources.

Below is an example of how you can reference image metadata in Azure:

```
data "azurerm_image" "example" {
  name                = "example-image"
  resource_group_name = "example-resources"
}
```

The azurerm_image data source allows you to reference the image data. Let us break it down. The name argument is the name of the image that you have created in the Azure resource group. The resource_group_name argument refers to the name of the resource group wherein the image is located.

To use this image when creating a virtual machine, you reference it like this:

```
resource "azurerm_linux_virtual_machine" "example" {
  name                 = "example-machine"
  resource_group_name  = azurerm_resource_group.example.name
  location             = azurerm_resource_group.example.location
  size                 = "Standard_F2"
  admin_username       = "adminuser"
  network_interface_id = azurerm_network_interface.example.id

  os_disk {
    caching            = "ReadWrite"
    storage_account_type = "Standard_LRS"
  }

  source_image_id = data.azurerm_image.example.id

  admin_ssh_key {
    username   = "adminuser"
    public_key = file("~/.ssh/id_rsa.pub")
  }

  disable_password_authentication = true
}
```

In the above given sample program, source_image_id is used to assign the image to the virtual machine, using the image id from the data source. However, if you'd like to use a public image from Azure Marketplace, you would need to use the azurerm_virtual_machine data source to reference it:

```
data "azurerm_platform_image" "example" {
```

```
  location  = "West Europe"
  publisher = "Canonical"
  offer     = "UbuntuServer"
  sku       = "16.04-LTS"
}

resource "azurerm_linux_virtual_machine" "example" {
  # ...
  source_image_reference {
    publisher = data.azurerm_platform_image.example.publisher
    offer     = data.azurerm_platform_image.example.offer
    sku       = data.azurerm_platform_image.example.sku
    version   = data.azurerm_platform_image.example.version
  }
  # ...
}
```

In this code, azurerm_platform_image is used to reference an image from Azure Marketplace. The publisher, offer, sku, and version fields are necessary to uniquely identify an image. Remember, always to refer to the Azure documentation or the specific image provider's instructions for the precise image metadata information you need to specify.

# Provision AKS Cluster

Provisioning an Azure Kubernetes Service (AKS) cluster using Terraform involves several steps, from setting up the necessary prerequisites to configuring the cluster properties, and finally creating the AKS cluster. Before provisioning the AKS cluster, ensure that you have installed the Azure CLI, Terraform, and kubectl on the machine. We should also have an active Azure account.

Following is an example that showcases the process:

## Setup Azure Provider

First, you'll need to set up the Azure provider:

```
provider "azurerm" {
  features {}
}
```

The azurerm provider is responsible for creating and managing resources on Azure.

## Define Resource Group

Next, we define a resource group:

```
resource "azurerm_resource_group" "example" {
  name     = "example-resources"
  location = "West Europe"
}
```

This block of code creates a resource group named "example-resources" in the "West Europe" region.

## Create AKS Networking Infrastructure

We will create a virtual network for our AKS cluster:

```
resource "azurerm_virtual_network" "example" {
  name                = "example-network"
  resource_group_name = azurerm_resource_group.example.name
  location            = azurerm_resource_group.example.location
  address_space       = ["10.1.0.0/16"]
}
```

This block creates a virtual network within the resource group, with the specified address space.

# Define Subnet for AKS Cluster

Define a subnet within the virtual network:

```
resource "azurerm_subnet" "example" {
  name                 = "example-subnet"
  resource_group_name  = azurerm_resource_group.example.name
  virtual_network_name = azurerm_virtual_network.example.name
  address_prefixes     = ["10.1.0.0/24"]
}
```

This code defines a subnet within the previously defined virtual network.

# Create AKS Cluster

The final step is to create the AKS cluster:

```
resource "azurerm_kubernetes_cluster" "example" {
  name                = "example-aks"
  location            = azurerm_resource_group.example.location
  resource_group_name = azurerm_resource_group.example.name
  dns_prefix          = "exampleaks"

  default_node_pool {
    name       = "default"
    node_count = 1
    vm_size    = "Standard_D2_v2"
    vnet_subnet_id = azurerm_subnet.example.id
  }

  identity {
    type = "SystemAssigned"
  }
}
```

This code block creates an AKS cluster named "example-aks" in the resource group we created. The dns_prefix is used to access the Kubernetes API server. The default_node_pool defines the properties of the default node pool, including the number of nodes (node_count), the VM size (vm_size), and the subnet where the node pool resides (vnet_subnet_id).

Finally, you can add additional configurations, like enabling Azure Active Directory, configuring networking plugins, enabling Azure monitor for containers, and more.

## Get Credentials for AKS Cluster

Once the cluster is set up, you'll need to get the credentials to connect to it. We can do this with Azure CLI:

```
az aks get-credentials --resource-group example-resources --name example-aks
```

We are now equipped to handle the AKS cluster through kubectl or the Kubernetes dashboard. Bear in mind, the creation of an AKS cluster might generate expenses. It's crucial to eliminate resources when they are no longer required to evade any unwarranted costs. In addition, you must take into account certain considerations like security, networking, and storage depending on your distinct use cases.

# Summary

In this chapter, we took a more in-depth look at some of the more complex Terraform principles and capabilities. To begin, we investigated various methods for developing re-usable, modular pieces of code that are referred to as Terraform modules. Modules enable infrastructure components to be bundled together and sent to several teams, which increases efficiency and facilitates collaboration. We are able to significantly enhance the pace of infrastructure deployments as well as the reliability of such deployments if we develop with modules rather than writing monolithic code.

Following that, we investigated the capabilities of HashiCorp Vault for safely managing sensitive information and secrets. Instead of relying on static keys and passwords, teams may take advantage of Vault's ability to generate ephemeral credentials in a dynamic manner. Both the security department and the operations department stand to gain a great deal from this increased level of automation and abstraction. Because the Vault plays such an important part in the building of modern infrastructure, a lot of ground was covered in it. After that, we shifted our focus to setting up a Kubernetes cluster on Microsoft Azure's cloud platform and walked through the process of creating an Azure Kubernetes Service

(AKS) cluster by specifying the necessary components such as resource groups, virtual networks, and subnets.

Finally, we investigated how Terraform may be used to manage the images and metadata of container containers. Terraform may be used to setup and deploy Kubernetes clusters and apps in the same way that it can be used to describe resources such as computing, network, and storage. We were able to witness directly how Terraform enables infrastructure teams by providing a standardized and uniform workflow across the stack, beginning with low-level cloud resources and progressing all the way up to container-based services.

# Thank You

# Index

# Epilogue

"As we reach the end of our journey with 'Terraform for Developers', we hope you have found this guide to be an enlightening experience, offering you a comprehensive understanding of Terraform's expansive capabilities. The purpose of this book was to empower you to become a professional Terraform developer, and we trust that the knowledge you gained and the skills you honed throughout will be instrumental in achieving this goal.

Through the course of the book, we dived deep into the world of Infrastructure as Code (IaC) and explored Terraform's integral role in it. We began with the basics, gradually exploring the tool's intricacies, offering you a clear, step-by-step understanding of Terraform's capabilities. We went from setting up Terraform and understanding its lifecycle, through managing various resources and handling errors, to exploring advanced topics like secrets management, networking, and testing.

We discussed the importance of effective secrets management using Azure Key Vault, and how it's crucial to modern, secure infrastructures. Through various examples and detailed explanations, we hoped to help you understand the practical aspects of managing secrets in real-world situations.

The chapters dedicated to networking with Terraform provided insights into managing critical networking components like VPCs, subnets, routing, and load balancers. These practical examples and step-by-step procedures aimed to help you understand the importance of networking in infrastructure management.

One of the key elements we focused on throughout the book is the value of testing in Terraform. By exploring unit, integration, validation, and compliance testing, we emphasized the need to ensure the reliability and robustness of the Terraform configurations.

The latter part of the book was dedicated to advanced topics, where we discussed managing Kubernetes resources, generating dynamic secrets with HashiCorp Vault, and provisioning an AKS cluster. The practical examples offered in these chapters were intended to help you navigate complex scenarios in real-world applications.

But the learning doesn't stop here. Terraform, like many other open-source tools, evolves continually, adapting to the changing landscape of infrastructure management and DevOps. We encourage you to keep exploring, experimenting, and building upon the foundational knowledge this book has provided. As you proceed, remember that the most important part of the learning process is not to get things right on the first try, but to learn from mistakes, persevere, and continually improve.

Finally, it's essential to remember that while Terraform is a powerful tool, it is just one part of a larger DevOps toolkit. Understanding how to effectively integrate Terraform into a larger CI/CD pipeline and automate infrastructure deployments is a crucial part of becoming a proficient Terraform developer.

We trust that 'Terraform for Developers' has given you the knowledge and skills you need to confidently use Terraform in the infrastructure management tasks. It's our hope that you're now ready to leverage Terraform's capabilities to their fullest extent and harness the power of Infrastructure as Code to simplify and streamline the infrastructure management workflows. The journey with Terraform is just beginning, and we're excited to see where it takes you. Happy coding!"

Made in the USA
Monee, IL
07 July 2026